Open Forum

ACADEMIC LISTENING AND SPEAKING

3

OXFORD
UNIVERSITY PRESS

198 Madison Avenue
New York, NY 10016 USA

Great Clarendon Street, Oxford OX2 6DP UK

Oxford University Press is a department of the University of Oxford.
It furthers the University's objective of excellence in research, scholarship,
and education by publishing worldwide in

Oxford New York

Auckland Cape Town Dar es Salaam Hong Kong Karachi
Kuala Lumpur Madrid Melbourne Mexico City Nairobi
New Delhi Shanghai Taipei Toronto

With offices in

Argentina Austria Brazil Chile Czech Republic France Greece
Guatemala Hungary Italy Japan Poland Portugal Singapore
South Korea Switzerland Thailand Turkey Ukraine Vietnam

OXFORD and OXFORD ENGLISH are registered trademarks of
Oxford University Press

© Oxford University Press 2007

Database right Oxford University Press (maker)

Senior Acquisitions Editor: Pietro Alongi
Editor: Rob Freire
Art Director: Maj-Britt Hagsted
Art Editor: Justine Eun
Production Manager: Shanta Persaud
Production Controller: Eve Wong

ISBN: 978 0 19 436113 2

Printed in Hong Kong.

10 9 8 7 6 5 4 3 2

Photography Credits:
*The publishers would like to thank the following for their permission to
reproduce photographs:*
Alamy: Bananastock, 74 (student taking test); Wally Bauman, 67
(psychologist); bobo, 68; Ashley Cooper, 103 (rescue cutters); Coston
Stock, 103 (bar code); eStock Photo, 102 (solar system); Robert Fried,
106; Jeff Greenberg, 71 (high jumper); Dennis Hallinan, 12 (Mona
Lisa); Bob Hosking, 62 (bird bower); D. Hurst, 103 (smoke detector);
Imagestate, 50 (earthquake); Olga Kolos, 110 (Hapshepsut's mortuary
palace); Mary Evans Picture Library, 12 (forged Mona Lisa); Photolibrary,
103 (cordless drill); Stockdisc Classic, 103 (joystick); Peter Titmuss, 30
(stair lift); vario images GmbH & Co. KG, 2 (Christmas tree purchase);
Associated Press: 43; CORBIS: Royalty-Free, 25 (woman using laptop);

Getty Images: Getty Images News, 2 (Christmas tree discarded), 6
(Toyota Prius); Getty Images Sport, 29 (Marlon Shirley, Paralympics
team); Taxi, 24 (men using handhelds); Time & Life Pictures, 110
(Hapshepsut statue); Inmagine: Digital Vision, 74 (woman stressed);
Image Source, 22 (man using cell phone); Photodisc, 31, 62 (bird bower);
Pixtal, 71 (soccer player); JupiterUnlimited: Comstock.com, 50 (tornado);
Goodshoot Image, 50 (field, desertification), 71 (cyclist); Photos.com, 23
(girls with camera phone), 50 (lightning bolt); Thinkstock.com, 6 (SUV),
67 (yoga); NASA Kennedy Space Center (NASA KSC): 102 (astronaut on
the moon); The National Gallery 2006: 17; SuperStock: Culver Pictures,
Inc., 39; SuperStock, Inc., 11;

Art Credits:
Arlene Boehm: 1, 38, 58, 97, 98; Marthe Roberts/Shea: 22, 81.

Acknowledgements

We would like to acknowledge Janet Aitchison and Pietro Alongi, who initiated the Open Forum series. We would also like to thank the editor Rob Freire, the art editor Justine Eun, the compositors Griffin Graphics, and the design project manager Niki Barolini for their hard work and dedication throughout the project. We would also like to express our gratitude to the following people for their support and feedback during the development of the book: Meg Baronian, Carolyn Carpenter, Barbara Harris, Barbara Mattingly, Karl Murphy, Michael Nieckoski, Abraham Noe-Hays, Adrianne Ochoa, Susan Olmstead and Scott Willis.

The publisher would like to thank the Hirshhorn Museum and Sculpture Garden, Smithsonian Institution, for permission to reproduce the following work:

Spiral Composition, 1946

Alexander Calder (1898–1976)

Gouache on paper (44.8 x 50.7 cm)

Hirshhorn Museum and Sculpture Garden, Smithsonian Institution, Gift of Joseph H. Hirshhorn, 1966.

Photographer: Lee Stalsworth.

Contents

Introduction

Welcome to *Open Forum,* a three-level listening and speaking skills series for English language learners who need practice in extended listening and discussion in preparation for academic work, or to attain a personal goal.

The series is structured around high-interest listening texts with an academic focus that engage and motivate learners. Chapters feature academic content areas such as History, Communication, or Psychology. The content areas are revisited as the series progresses, ensuring that learners recycle and extend the ideas and vocabulary of each topic. Focused practice in listening and speaking skills is integrated into each chapter.

Open Forum 3 is for learners at the **high-intermediate** level.

Features of *Open Forum*

Listening Skills

- Each chapter introduces and practices a specific listening skill (e.g., listening for main ideas, identifying examples, identifying important points).

- Listening selections are adapted from authentic sources. They are carefully chosen to engage learners and teachers and to stimulate discussion.

- A wide variety of texts—including lectures, radio interviews, news reports, and informal conversations—ensures learners practice listening to a range of audio formats.

- Listening comprehension tasks provide opportunities for extensive and intensive listening, which becomes more challenging as learners move through the series.

Speaking Skills

- Each chapter introduces and practices one specific speaking skill (e.g., elaborating, asking for clarification, giving opinions).

- Speaking practice sections in each chapter provide opportunities for extended discussion on the chapter theme.

- Abundant opportunities for interaction in pairs, groups, and as a class ensure student participation.

Vocabulary

- Vocabulary sections introduce key lexical items associated with the chapter theme. The sections also highlight word-building, collocations, and multi-word verbs.

Pronunciation

- Pronunciation sections raise learners' awareness of features of natural spoken English, such as stress, rhythm, intonation, and linking.

MP3 Component

- Downloadable audio files (in MP3 format) and worksheets for every chapter are available on the *Open Forum* Web site www.oup.com/elt/openforum. Each downloadable selection complements the topic in the corresponding chapter, and provides learners with opportunities for extended listening practice in the content area. The listening selections can be used independently, or in a language lab setting.

Assessment

- Progress Tests (available in the *Answer Key* and *Test Booklet*) enable teachers to check learners' progress and allow learners to demonstrate mastery of the strategies they have studied.

Unit Format

1. Introducing the Topic

This section introduces the topic of the chapter, activates learners' background knowledge, and builds interest. Learners complete a quiz, answer discussion questions, look at photographs, or carry out a short survey.

Teaching Tip: Use this section to get learners thinking and speaking about the chapter theme. Have them work in pairs or groups to maximize their speaking opportunities.

2. Listening Practice

This is the first of two major listening opportunities in each chapter. Each listening section includes five sub-sections:

- **Preparing to Listen**

  Here, learners are given specific preparation for the text that they are going to hear. Learners read and discuss information specific to the piece; at this point, new vocabulary may be introduced to facilitate listening.

  Teaching Tip: Heighten student interest and anticipation by having them predict what speakers will say. Leave some questions unanswered; this will motivate learners to listen more carefully.

- **Listening for Main Ideas**

  This stage ensures that learners are able to identify the main idea of a text. The listening task encourages learners to listen to the entire recording once through, without stopping, and to pick out the general gist of the text.

  Teaching Tip: Read through the directions for the task before learners listen. Check that they understand the vocabulary in the task and know what they have to do. Encourage them to focus only on the listening task as they listen. After they listen, have learners compare their answers, and check as a class.

- **Listening for More Detail**

  In this section, learners practice listening for specific details. As the series progresses, learners move from reacting with a minimal response (e.g., deciding whether a statement is true or false) to making more extended notes (e.g., filling in a chart). They are also guided to use context to work out unknown vocabulary.

  Teaching Tip: Go through the questions before learners listen, and check that they understand what they are being asked. Then play the recording. Learners may already be able to answer some of the questions. Acknowledge this fact, but do not confirm right or wrong answers at this point: encourage learners to listen a second time to check their answers. After they have listened again, ask learners to compare their answers, and check as a class. If learners have difficulty with one or more of the questions, replay the relevant section of the recording as necessary.

- **Thinking and Speaking**

  At this point, learners are encouraged to respond to the ideas in the text, synthesize what they have heard, and apply it to their own experience. Learners also get an opportunity for speaking practice on the chapter theme.

  Teaching Tip: Learners can discuss the questions in pairs, small groups, or as a class. Give them time to think before asking for answers. Encourage them to refer to the listening transcript if appropriate. The tasks are designed to be flexible and can take as little as a few minutes, or as long as 20–30 minutes, depending on class and teacher preference.

- **Focus on the Listening Skill**

  This section raises learners' awareness of listening skills and strategies, and provides focused training in those skills. The *Listening Skill* boxes introduce three types of listening skills:

  a) pre-listening skills (e.g., activating background knowledge) are introduced before learners listen to the text;

  b) while-listening skills (e.g., identifying main ideas) are introduced and practiced as learners listen;

  c) detailed listening skills (e.g., working out unknown vocabulary) are practiced after learners have grasped the main points.

  Teaching Tip: Read the information in the Listening Skill box aloud as the learners follow along. Check that they understand. Then have them complete the tasks alone or with a partner. After they listen, have learners compare their answers, and check as a class.

3. Vocabulary

The vocabulary section introduces key items of vocabulary that are useful for the topic, and provides written and oral practice of the items. Where necessary, *FYI* boxes highlight relevant information.

Teaching Tip: Read the information in the FYI box, if there is one, aloud as the learners follow along. Check

that learners understand. Then ask learners to complete the tasks alone or with a partner.

4. Listening Practice

This section provides a second listening opportunity. The text in this section is longer than the first text, to give learners practice in extended listening. The text is usually of a different type from the first text (e.g., a lecture vs. a radio interview). The sequence of tasks is the same as in the first listening section, without the specific focus on a listening skill.

Teaching Tip: See previous Listening Practice.

5. Pronunciation

Learners are offered practice in listening for and understanding features of natural spoken English such as stress, linking, weak forms, and verb endings. Learners practice focused listening to identify stress and intonation and to pick out words and complete sentences. As in the *Vocabulary* section, *FYI* boxes provide relevant instruction.

Teaching Tip: Read the information in the FYI box, if there is one, aloud as the learners follow along. Check that learners understand. Then ask learners to complete the tasks alone or with a partner.

6. Speaking Skills

This section raises learners' awareness of a specific speaking skill or strategy, such as asking for clarification or taking time to think. These are presented in *Speaking Skill* boxes. Learners listen to a short text that exemplifies the skill or strategy in question.

Teaching Tip: Read the information in the Speaking Skill box aloud as the learners follow along. Check that learners understand. Then ask learners to complete the tasks alone or with partner.

7. Speaking Practice

This section provides an extensive, guided speaking activity on the theme of the chapter, and encourages learners to use the skill learned in the previous section. The activity is carefully staged to maximize speaking; for example, learners might first make notes individually, then discuss the topic with a partner, and finally move into group or class discussion.

Teaching Tip: Allow plenty of time for this activity. Ask learners to gather and note down their ideas; this will ensure that they have enough to say in the speaking stage. If necessary, remind learners to use the speaking skill from the previous section.

8. Taking Skills Further

The chapter concludes with suggestions to increase learners' awareness of listening and speaking skills, and ideas for listening and speaking practice outside the classroom.

Teaching Tip: The task can usually be checked in the next class. Many of the activities can be expanded into a project, if desired.

ABOUT THIS CHAPTER	
Topic:	Conservation
Listening Texts:	Talk on recycling Christmas trees; radio program about biodiesel
Listening Skill Focus:	Working out unknown vocabulary
Speaking Skill Focus:	Explaining a process
Vocabulary:	Words related to the environment
Pronunciation:	The –es ending

1 | **INTRODUCING THE TOPIC**

1. Work with a partner. Read the quiz about ecological concerns. Discuss possible
answers to the questions. (The answers are at the bottom of the page.)

ENVIRONMENTAL QUIZ

1. What produces more oxygen
   than any other source?
   a. microscopic ocean plants
   b. plants in rainforests

2. How often does the population
   double in number?
   a. every 39 years
   b. every 300 years

3. How many of the aluminum cans
   produced now are recycled?
   a. 95%
   b. 50%

4. What is the main source of
   air pollution?
   a. factory exhaust
   b. automobile exhaust

5. How many people live in areas
   where the air is potentially
   unhealthy to breathe?
   a. A million
   b. Over a billion

6. How much paper is used each
   year in the U.S., per person?
   a. 50 pounds (23kg)
   b. 600 pounds (272kg)

2. Check your answers to the quiz. Which fact surprises you most?

Answers: 1. a, 2. a, 3. b, 4. b, 5. b, 6. b

A Preparing to Listen

Work with a partner. Look at the pictures and discuss the questions below.

1. Every year in the United States, approximately 33 million real trees are bought for the Christmas holidays. What do you think might happen to those trees after the holidays?

2. Where you live, where is garbage taken when it leaves your home? What happens to it?

B Listening for Main Ideas

Listen to a talk about a program that uses Christmas trees. As you listen, write *T* for true or *F* for false for each item.

_____ 1. Christmas trees are being used in lakes and rivers as a place for fish to live and grow.

_____ 2. There are usually many natural places for fish to hide and grow in lakes and waterways.

_____ 3. This program is happening in only one or two states.

_____ 4. This program is expensive and difficult to maintain.

C Listening for More Detail

Listen to the talk again. Then choose the correct answer for each question.

1. Who is the person giving the talk?
   a. She is a biologist.
   b. She is a park ranger.

2. How are trees being used as homes for fish?
   a. The trees grow underwater.
   b. The trees are dropped into lakes and rivers.

3. Why do fish need these trees?
   a. They need a place to hide from bigger fish.
   b. They eat the leaves.

4. Why do many lakes not have natural vegetation in them?
   a. The vegetation has died.
   b. Many lakes are manmade.

5. Where are some of the places the practice of reusing Christmas trees is taking place?
   a. California and Maryland
   b. Colorado and Maryland

6. How many trees are officials and fishermen planning to sink in the Colorado River?
   a. 700
   b. 4,000

7. Why have some fishermen dropped their own trees in lakes?
   a. They hope the trees will attract fish.
   b. They are required to do this by law.

D Focus on the Listening Skill: Working Out Unknown Vocabulary

LISTENING SKILL

If you don't know what a word or expression means, pay attention to the words around it and the general meaning of the sentence. Also, use your background knowledge to help you. This can help you work out the meaning of the unfamiliar word.

🎧 1. **Read and listen to the extract from the talk. Look at the example below to see how the meaning of *fry* was worked out.**

Young fish, or fry, and small fish living in bodies of water that have no vegetation are particularly vulnerable to larger predators—like bigger fish or other creatures who are hunting for food.

Fry probably means ____.
a. young fish
b. small lakes

How did you know? <u>Because "young fish" was next to "fry" so it's another way of</u>

<u>saying it.</u>

🎧 2. **Listen to the extract again. Then choose the correct meaning for *predators* and explain the reason for your choice.**

Predators probably means ____.
a. fishermen
b. animals that hunt and eat other animals

How did you know? _____

🎧 3. **For each item, listen to the extract and try to work out the meaning of the word in italics. Compare answers with a partner and discuss the reasons for your choices.**

1. *Habitat* probably means ____.
   a. a place to fish
   b. a place to live

2. A *reef* is probably ____.
   a. a dam
   b. an underwater line of rocks or sand

3. *Debris* probably means ____.
   a. fish and other animals
   b. the remains of something, like leaves, sticks, or branches

4. *Sink* probably means ____.
   a. cut something down
   b. drop something below the surface of the water

E Thinking and Speaking

Discuss the questions in small groups.

1. Do you think it is worthwhile to create fish habitats with Christmas trees? Why or why not?
2. Do you know of any other creative solutions to environmental problems?

3 | VOCABULARY: Words Related to the Environment

Read the following information from a Web site. Then match each word in bold with the correct definition.

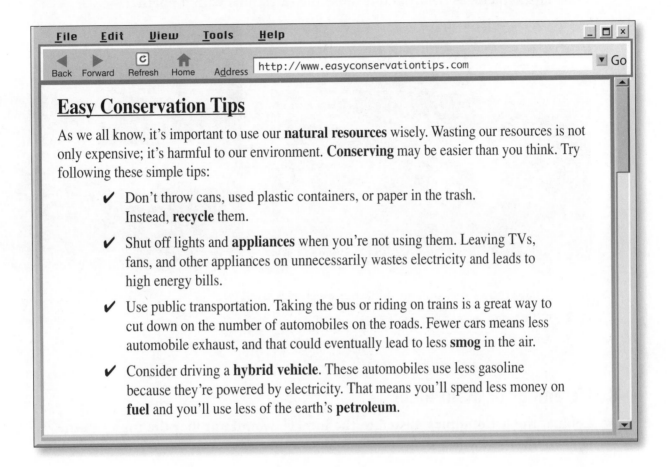

_c_ 1. recycle	a. to protect something or keep it from being wasted; save
___ 2. conserve	b. a mixture of fog and smoke, or some other pollution in the air
___ 3. natural resource	c. to process a used material so that it can be used again
___ 4. appliance	d. something valuable, like water or oil, that is produced by nature
___ 5. fuel	e. oil that is produced naturally by the earth
___ 6. hybrid vehicle	f. something that is burned to provide power or heat
___ 7. smog	g. an automobile that uses both gasoline and electricity
___ 8. petroleum	h. an electrical machine that is used in the home

A Preparing to Listen

Look at the pictures below and discuss the questions with a partner.

1. What kind of fuel do you think these vehicles use?

2. Which one uses more fuel?

3. What are the advantages and disadvantages of owning each vehicle?

B Listening for Main Ideas

Look at the list of topics. Listen to the interview and number the topics in the order they are discussed.

_____ a. Where biodiesel comes from

_____ b. Who created a vehicle that ran on ethanol

_____ c. Disadvantages to using biodiesel

_____ d. Safety of biodiesel

C Listening for More Detail

Read the questions. Then listen to the interview again. As you listen, note your answers to the questions. Then compare answers with a partner. Listen again if necessary.

1. Who is Rudolph Diesel?

_____

_____

2. Why is there renewed interest in alternative fuels?

_____

_____

3. What must you do so that your car can use biodiesel?

_____

_____

4. What are some benefits to using biodiesel?

_____

_____

5. Where is biodiesel currently being used?

_____

_____

6. What are two disadvantages to using biodiesel?

_____

_____

D Working Out Unknown Vocabulary

Listen to the extracts from the program. Listen for the words and expressions in italics. Choose the correct meaning for each word or expression.

1. *Back on the scene* probably means _____.
   a. in the past, a long time ago
   b. popular again

2. *Modify* probably means _____.
   a. alter or change something
   b. fix or repair something

3. *Backing* probably means _____.
   a. selling
   b. supporting financially

E Thinking and Speaking

Work in groups. Discuss the questions.

1. Do you think it is important to use alternative fuels like biodiesel? Explain your answer.

2. Would you use an alternative fuel like biodiesel?

3. Why aren't alternative fuels like biodiesel more popular? Why don't more people use them?

5 | **PRONUNCIATION:** The –*es* ending

The –*es* ending is sometimes pronounced as an extra syllable, and sometimes it is not. The –*es* ending adds an extra syllable to a noun or a verb that ends in the following sounds: /s/, /z/, /j/, /ch/, or /sh/. With words that do not end in these sounds, the –*es* ending is not pronounced as an extra syllable.

1. Listen to these pairs of words. Tap your hand or a pen with each syllable you hear. Notice how the –*es* ending adds an extra syllable.

1 Syllable	2 Syllables
watch	watch**es**
page	pag**es**
class	class**es**
wash	wash**es**
use	us**es**

2 Syllables	3 Syllables
resource	resourc**es**
practice	practic**es**
reduce	reduc**es**
approach	approach**es**

2. Listen to the extracts from the interview. Circle the word you hear.

1. use / uses

2. shortage / shortages

3. approach / approaches

4. school bus / school buses

5. reduce / reduces

6. increase / increases

3. Look at the words below. Check each word where you think the –*es* ending is pronounced as an extra syllable. Then listen to the words and check your answers.

_____ 1. engines   _____ 5. produces

_____ 2. automobiles   _____ 6. invests

_____ 3. taxes   _____ 7. embraces

_____ 4. gases   _____ 8. converts

6 | SPEAKING SKILLS: Explaining a Process

SPEAKING SKILL

When you are explaining a process to someone, or showing someone how to operate something, use words and expressions like the ones below to explain the sequence of steps.

First of all, . . .	Next, . . .
First, . . .	After that, . . .
Second, . . .	Later, . . .
Then, . . .	Finally, . . .

1. Listen to this short explanation of how the Greenhouse Effect works. Number the steps in the order in which they occur.

_____ a. Some of it is immediately reflected off the atmosphere back out into space.

_____ b. Sunlight hits the earth's atmosphere.

_____ c. However, most of the energy enters the atmosphere and is absorbed by various features on earth.

_____ d. But greenhouse gases trap most of this released energy.

_____ e. Energy radiates back down warming up the earth's surface.

_____ f. This keeps the earth warm and a comfortable place for life to exist.

_____ g. This energy is eventually released off the earth's surface.

2. Which expressions does the speaker use to explain the sequence of steps?

7 | SPEAKING PRACTICE

1. Pick one of the topics below or a topic of your own. Practice explaining the process to a partner.

- How a car engine works
- How to download music from the internet
- How to make a blanket
- How to plant a (flower, vegetable, container) garden
- How a solar eclipse happens

2. Role play in front of the class. You are a TV show host. Explain one of the processes above to your class "audience."

8 | TAKING SKILLS FURTHER

Watch a TV cooking show. Listen for sequencing expressions that the host uses to explain how to cook something. Write down the ones you hear. Discuss your findings in the next class.

 For additional listening practice on the topic of natural resources and conservation, go to the *Open Forum* Web site (www.oup.com/elt/openforum) and follow the links.

CHAPTER 2 Visual Art

1 INTRODUCING THE TOPIC

1. Look at the painting and discuss the questions with a partner.

Vincent Van Gogh's Fifteen Sunflowers in a Vase sold for
$40 million dollars in 1987.

1. Why do you think someone would pay so much for artwork?

2. If you had enough money, would you spend that much on a painting or sculpture? What would you buy?

2. Look at the list of art forms below and add any others that you can think of to the list. Then answer the questions. Compare your answers with a partner.

architecture	opera
ballet	poetry
classical music	sculpture
hip hop	watercolor painting
jazz	_____
modern dance	_____
oil painting	_____

1. Which of the art forms above are you interested in? What do you know about them?

2. Do you enjoy going to art museums?

3. Is it important to study the arts in school? Why or why not?

2 LISTENING PRACTICE

A Preparing to Listen

1. Look at these paintings. One of them is the real Mona Lisa, by Leonardo da Vinci, and the other is a forgery, a copy of the original. Can you tell which one is the real Mona Lisa? (The answer is at the bottom of the page.)

2. You are going to hear a conversation about art forgeries. Before you listen, discuss these questions with a partner.

1. Why would someone paint a forgery of a famous painting?

2. How do you think an art expert can tell the difference between an original piece of art and a forgery?

Answer: The painting on the right is the real Mona Lisa.

B Listening for Main Ideas

Listen to the conversation. Then answer the questions. Compare your answers with a partner.

1. What was the TV program about?

2. Why is it sometimes difficult to tell the difference between an original piece of art and a forgery?

C Listening for More Detail

1. Listen to the conversation again. Write *T* for true or *F* for false for each statement. Then compare answers with a partner. Listen again if necessary.

_____ 1. Buyers should learn as much as they can about the artist's style.

_____ 2. Buyers should talk to the painting's previous owners.

_____ 3. Holding a black light to a painting may reveal if it is a copy.

_____ 4. The chemical composition of the paint may help determine if a painting is real or not.

_____ 5. Comparing fingerprints left in paint helps in detecting a forgery.

_____ 6. It's always possible to identify a forged painting.

_____ 7. Most public and private collections have no forgeries at all.

_____ 8. Some forgeries have become valuable themselves.

2. Work in pairs. Discuss why the false statements are false. Then correct them to make them true.

D Thinking and Speaking

Work in pairs. Discuss these questions.

1. In your own words, explain some of the ways that art experts can detect a forgery.

2. Have you ever bought a piece of artwork? What is it? Where did you get it?

3. Do you admire forgers? Why or why not?

E Focus on the Listening Skill: Reflecting on Listening

LISTENING SKILL

It is helpful to think about what skills are necessary to be a good listener and to practice these skills as much as possible. This will improve your ability to understand what others are saying and will make you feel more confident when listening.

1. **Work with a partner. Discuss the following questions.**

    1. When you are listening to a lecture or a lesson, what do you do to help you understand?

    2. If you are having difficulty understanding someone, what do you do?

    3. How do you prefer to practice listening to English? Number the activities below in order of preference. 1 = Favorite. 5 = Least favorite.

        _____ Watching TV or movies

        _____ Listening to music

        _____ Talking to friends or people at work or school

        _____ Studying about listening skills in English class

        _____ Other: _____

2. **Look at the following strategies for becoming a better listener. Then look back at sections A through D on pages 12 and 13. Which strategy did you use in each section?**

    1. When you listen, focus on the main ideas, not the details. _____

    2. Think about what you already know about the topic before you listen. _____

    3. Listen for specific information that you want to find out. _____

    4. After you listen, summarize what you heard. _____

3. **In this book you will have the opportunity to practice different skills and strategies to help you improve your listening abilities. Look at the list of listening skills in the Table of Contents. Which chapters teach the strategies listed in exercise 2 above?**

3 | VOCABULARY: Words Related to Art Crime

1. **Read the sentences. Match each word in bold with a definition below.**

    _____ 1. Buying diamonds ourselves, we couldn't tell if they were **authentic** or not. They might not be real.

    _____ 2. The buyers took the jewelry to a **reputable** gem expert. He appraised it at a fair value.

    _____ 3. It's against the law to pass **counterfeit** money. If you get some you just have to keep it.

    _____ 4. A **forgery** of a Picasso painting was sold at auction for many hundreds of thousands of dollars. Experts later verified it was a fake.

    _____ 5. Experts use various chemical analyses to **detect** forgeries.

    a. not real
    b. a fake, a copy that is presented as something it is not in order to trick people

    c. trustworthy, honest, having a good reputation
    e. find, discover
    d. genuine, real, true

2. **Read the text about a famous forger. Fill in each blank with one of the words in bold from exercise 1.**

When did the business of (1) _____ begin? Many people agree

it started long ago in ancient Rome when selling (2) _____ statues of

Greek sculpture became profitable. Since then, many different things have been forged:

coins, stamps, documents, jewelry, and of course, paintings.

One of the most well known forgers in recent history was Han van Meegeren, a

struggling Dutch artist. He produced and sold forgeries of paintings by the great artist

Vermeer for many years in the early 20th century. Originally, his purpose was not to profit

from his works, but to embarrass art critics. No one (3) _____ his

deception, until one of his pieces was discovered in the property of the Nazi Herman Göring

after WWII. Ironically, it turns out Göring used counterfeit money to pay for the forged

painting!

While trying to clear his name as a Nazi sympathizer, van Meegeren explained that

he had forged the Vermeer. Authorities didn't believe him, so under arrest, he proved his

skill by creating a "new" Vermeer. The public and police were stunned. He was eventually

charged with forgery rather than treason, but instead of going to prison, he died soon

after his trial. By the way, there are only about thirty (4) _____, or real

Vermeers that exist today.

Stories of successful forgers like this abound in the art world, and serve as a cautionary

tale for anyone interested in investing in art. Be careful; make your investment at

(5) _____ auction houses. If you think you have a one of a kind

masterpiece, you may only have a very good copy.

3. **Work with a partner and answer the following questions.**

1. Why did Han van Meegeren become famous?

2. Han van Meegeren painted forgeries to embarrass art critics. How did his forgeries embarrass the critics?

4 LISTENING PRACTICE

A Preparing to Listen

You are going to hear a tour guide in an art museum. Before you listen, look at the list of artists' names below. Check the names that you know. Can you name any of their famous works? Do you know any other famous painters?

_____ Leonardo da Vinci

_____ Michelangelo

_____ Giotto

_____ Vermeer

_____ Albrecht Durer

_____ Botticelli

_____ Van Gogh

B Listening for Main Ideas

Listen to the talk at a museum. After you listen, answer the question.

What is the theory suggested in the lecture? Re-state it in your own words.

C Listening for More Detail

Listen again. Write·*T* for true or *F* for false for each statement. Then compare answers with a partner. Listen again if necessary.

_____ 1. Fifteenth and sixteenth century artists were able to paint details realistically.

_____ 2. A camera obscura projects an image on a surface.

_____ 3. Experts have proven that Vermeer used a camera obscura.

_____ 4. A camera obscura requires a very dark room and bright daylight.

_____ 5. The people in Vermeer's work look as they would in a photograph.

_____ 6. Vermeer often sketched his work before starting to paint.

_____ 7. There is evidence in his Family Portrait, that Lorenzo Lotto may have used a camera obscura.

D Working Out Unknown Vocabulary

Listen to extracts from the talk. Listen for the words in italics. Choose the correct meaning for each word.

1. *Tapestry* probably means _____.
   a. something made of glass
   b. cloth with colored threads woven into it

2. *Optical* probably means _____.
   a. related to the eye or vision
   b. detailed

3. *Phenomenon* probably means _____.
   a. portrait or painting
   b. an interesting or remarkable occurrence

4. *Primitive* probably means _____.
   a. from an early stage of development; not advanced
   b. complicated

E Thinking and Speaking

Work with a partner. Discuss these questions.

1. How do artists nowadays use modern technology to create art?

2. Do you think artists who use modern technology to manipulate images in their work are as skilled as those who don't use technology?

5 PRONUNCIATION: Word Stress in Nouns and Verbs

 Many two-syllable nouns and verbs are spelled the same way, but are pronounced differently. Usually, the stress is on the first syllable in nouns and on the second syllable in verbs. For example, the noun *record* is pronounced **rec**ord and the verb *record* is pronounced re**cord**.

1. Listen to four extracts from the lecture. Circle the word you hear.

1. However, some researchers <u>sus</u>pect / sus<u>pect</u> these artists may have had help.

2. We have probably all been in awe of the old masters; those pre-Renaissance painters of the 15th and 16th centuries with their ability to capture minute details: threads on a tapestry or silk dresses, reflections off pitchers, glasses, chandeliers and other metal <u>ob</u>jects / ob<u>jects</u>.

3. It would have taken a very long time to <u>pro</u>ject / pro<u>ject</u> an image with such detailed accuracy.

4. In Vermeer's work, the evidence, after much <u>re</u>search / re<u>search</u>, these experts say, is in paintings with more than one figure . . .

5. If there are no more questions on this <u>sub</u>ject / sub<u>ject</u>, let's begin the tour.

2. **Listen to the sentences. Circle the word that you hear.**

1.	contract	contract
2.	record	record
3.	conflict	conflict
4.	permit	permit
5.	reject	reject

3. **With a partner, practice saying the sentences in exercise 1 and the pairs of words in exercise 2. Are you putting the stress on the correct syllable?**

6 SPEAKING SKILLS: Using Expressions to Show Interest

> **SPEAKING SKILL**
>
> When someone is talking, you can use expressions to show that you are interested in what they're saying. Note that you can also nod (move your head up and down) to show that you are listening and you understand.

1. **Listen to three short exchanges. Listen to what the second speaker says to express interest. Write down the replies.**

1. Man: I heard this interesting program on the radio.

   Woman: _____?

2. Woman: Did you know some artists may have used camera-like devices when they painted?

   Man: _____? _____.

3. Woman: They projected images on a canvas.

   Man: _____? _____!

2. Look at the list of expressions below. Read the conversations and write an appropriate expression of interest. More than one answer is possible.

Really?	That's amazing / incredible / interesting.
You did?	Interesting.
You were?	That's too bad.
Uh-huh.	I'm sorry to hear that.
Is that right?	Wow!
That's good.	

Charles: I missed the field trip to the museum yesterday.

Maureen: _____

Charles: Yeah, my alarm didn't go off when it was supposed to.

Maureen: _____

Charles: I went back and looked at the exhibit today, though.

Maureen: _____

Charles: The Renaissance paintings impressed me a lot.

Maureen: _____

Charles: Now, I just need to decide what to write my report on.

3. Work with a partner. Practice the conversation out loud. Can you think of any other expressions of interest to add to the list?

7 SPEAKING PRACTICE

1. Look at the list of events below. Check any of the events that have happened to you.

_____ Met a famous person

_____ Had a serious car accident

_____ Had your wallet stolen

_____ Found money somewhere

_____ Been on TV

_____ Flown first-class on an airplane

_____ Seen a UFO

_____ Gotten lost somewhere

_____ Had a strange dream

2. Work with a partner. Tell each other about the experiences you've had. Respond to your partner appropriately using some of the expressions on page 19.

3. Answer the questions. Then discuss one of your answers with a partner.

    1. What's the strangest experience you've ever had?

    2. Think about a time when you were scared. What happened? What did you do?

    3. Think about one of the best experiences in your life. What happened?

8 | TAKING SKILLS FURTHER

Take a tour at a local museum. Listen and watch how the tour members express interest in what the tour guide is saying. Write down any new expressions that you hear and bring them to class.

For additional listening practice on the topic of visual art, go to the *Open Forum* Web site (www.oup.com/elt/openforum) and follow the links.

ABOUT THIS CHAPTER

Topics:	Cell phone etiquette; the Internet and relationships
Listening Texts:	Conversation about cell phones; radio commentary on the Internet and relationships
Listening Skill Focus:	Listening for main ideas
Speaking Skill Focus:	Reflecting on speaking
Vocabulary:	Expressions with *can't*
Pronunciation:	Voiced and voiceless consonants

1 | INTRODUCING THE TOPIC

1. Complete the survey. Then compare your answers as a class. What are the three most frequent activities for your class? What are the three least frequent activities?

How do you spend your home time?

Number the following activities according to how frequently you do them when you are home.
1 = Most Frequent. 10 = Least Frequent.

- [ ] Reading
- [ ] Surfing the Internet
- [ ] Emailing friends
- [ ] Visiting chat rooms or discussion boards
- [ ] Talking with family members
- [ ] Playing video games
- [ ] Talking on the phone
- [ ] Text messaging
- [ ] Listening to music
- [ ] Watching TV or DVDs

2 | LISTENING PRACTICE

A Preparing to Listen

Many people believe that using a cell phone in public can be a problem. Look at the list below. With a partner, discuss whether you think each activity is acceptable or unacceptable, and why.

- Using a cell phone on the bus
- Taking someone's picture with a phone without the person knowing it
- Answering a cell phone at work
- Answering a cell phone in a movie theater
- Talking on the phone while driving
- Posting pictures from a phone on the Internet without permission

B Listening for Main Ideas

Listen to the conversation. Then answer the questions.

1. What does Jessica want? _____

2. How does her mother feel about what Jessica wants? _____
_____

3. At the end of their discussion, does Jessica's mother let Jessica get what she wants?
_____

C Listening for More Detail

Listen again. Check the reasons that Jessica and her mother each give for their own points of view.

Jessica:

_____ Her friend has a camera phone.

_____ She wants to use her phone in school.

_____ She wants to take pictures of books and magazines.

_____ She wants a camera phone in case she has a car accident.

Jessica's mother:

_____ Jessica already has a cell phone.

_____ She is worried that Jessica won't pay for a new phone.

_____ Jessica uses her cell phone too much now.

_____ She doesn't believe Jessica will use good judgment if she has a camera phone.

D Thinking and Speaking

Work in small groups. Discuss these questions.

1. If you were Jessica's mother, would you get her a new camera phone? Why or why not?

2. What is the strangest place you've seen anyone use a cell phone?

3. Have you ever had to use your cell phone for an emergency? Describe the situation.

4. Do you talk on your phone while you drive? Do you think this is dangerous? Explain your answer.

2 VOCABULARY: Expressions with *Can't*

1. A few expressions with *can't* have special meanings. Read the following sentences and underline the two-word expressions with *can't*.

   1. I <u>can't stand</u> the traffic here. It's horrible!

   2. I can't believe she said that. She should have kept it to herself.

   3. We can't afford a new laptop. It's too expensive.

   4. It can't be Mark. He's in Germany right now.

2. Write each underlined expression from above next to the correct definition below.

   1. _____: to be surprised or shocked at something

   2. _____: to not have enough money to buy something

   3. _____: to be impossible

   4. _____: to dislike something strongly

3. Read the sentences below and circle the correct expression for each sentence.

   1. My wife lost her job recently, so we <u>can't stand / can't afford</u> to go on vacation this year.

   2. We <u>can't believe / can't stand</u> that she lost her job. Her bosses have always said she's an excellent worker.

3. When it happened, my wife thought, "This <u>can't afford / can't be</u> happening!

4. My wife <u>can't stand / can't believe</u> not working, so she is getting depressed.

5. I <u>can't afford / can't stand</u> seeing her like this. I worry about her a lot, and I get depressed too.

4 | LISTENING PRACTICE

A Preparing to Listen

You are going to listen to a radio commentary about the Internet and personal relationships. Before you listen, discuss the questions below with a partner.

1. How do you think computers and the Internet can improve relationships between people (friends, family members, neighbors, co-workers.)?

2. How do you think the Internet can impact relationships in a negative way?

B Focus on the Listening Skill: Listening for Main Ideas

> **LISTENING SKILL**
>
> When you listen to a program or any other kind of presentation, don't expect to grasp every piece of information the first time you listen. Instead, whenever possible, use the first listen to get the gist or main ideas.

1. Here are some comments from language learners describing the ways they identify main ideas. Add a comment of your own and then discuss the comments with a partner.

   1. I find the main idea is often the first point in a paragraph.

   2. Main ideas are stated in broad terms and then followed by details or examples.

   3. Often, main ideas are repeated more than once.

   4. Your comment: _____

2. Read the statements below. Then listen to the radio program about the Internet and relationships. After you listen, check the 4 main ideas that are presented. (All these ideas are mentioned, but only 4 of them are main ideas.)

_____ The Internet encourages more frequent contact with friends and family than the phone.

_____ Families often use the Internet to address serious matters.

_____ People who are disabled or housebound can develop cyber relationships and feel less isolated.

_____ People cannot really get to know someone online.

_____ Children can be put in dangerous situations as a result of online activity.

_____ Excessive use of the Internet can have negative effects.

_____ People are less polite online.

_____ The Internet can help us build relationships, but it can also lead to isolation.

C Listening for More Detail

Read the questions and answer as many as you can. Then listen again and complete your responses. Compare answers with a partner.

1. How can the Internet help build relationships with friends and family?

_____

_____

2. What benefits does the Internet offer to those who are disabled or housebound?

_____

_____

3. What are some advantages of Internet dating over face-to-face meetings?

_____

_____

4. What are some of the negative aspects of meeting people online?

_____

_____

5. What should parents do to protect children from online predators?

_____

_____

6. Why is it easier to be rude online than in face-to-face meetings?

_____

_____

D Working Out Unknown Vocabulary

Work with a partner. Listen to the extracts from the radio program. Listen for the words and expressions in italics. Then choose the correct meaning for each word or expression.

1. *Cyber* probably means _____.
   a. related to computers or the Internet
   b. new

2. *Posing as* probably means _____.
   a. pretending to be something or someone
   b. meeting someone

3. *Monitor* probably means _____.
   a. ignore
   b. watch or check carefully

4. *Prevalent* probably means _____.
   a. very rare
   b. very common

E Thinking and Speaking

Work in a small group and discuss one of the following questions.

1. For what purposes do you use the Internet? List as many purposes as you can think of.

2. Is information on the Internet trustworthy? Explain your answer.

3. In what new ways do you think the Internet will be used in the future?

5 | PRONUNCIATION: Voiced and Voiceless Consonants

Some consonants in English are voiced and others are voiceless. When we pronounce voiced consonants, like the sounds /z/, /v/, /b/, /d/, /g/, and /j/, our vocal cords vibrate. For example, when saying the word *love,* the vocal cords vibrate when we make the consonant /v/, and this creates a buzzing sound. Our vocal cords do not vibrate when we pronounce voiceless consonants, like /s/, /f/, /p/, /t/, /k/ and /ch/. Hearing the difference between voiced and voiceless consonants can help you understand some words more accurately.

1. Listen and repeat the following words. Notice how the last consonant in each word is voiced.

save	raise
live	plays
lose	have

2. Listen and repeat these words. Notice how the last consonant in each word is voiceless.

safe	race
life	place
loose	half

3. Work with a partner. Practice saying the following sentences.

1. His brother plays video games all day.
2. My favorite place is home.
3. I like to visit live chat rooms.
4. I had the time of my life.
5. The Internet is not always safe.
6. Using email helps me to save time.

6 | SPEAKING SKILLS: Reflecting on Speaking

SPEAKING SKILL

Think about your progress, strengths, and needs in speaking. This can help you identify next steps to focus on to improve your speaking skills.

Look at these statements from language learners commenting on their experiences with speaking. Then add a comment of your own.

1. I can usually state a point clearly, but when I provide details or defend my position, I have difficulty.

2. I need more time to process my ideas than other students. So sometimes, when I am ready to speak, the discussion has moved on to another topic.

3. I don't like expressing my opinion.

4. Your comment: _____

   _____

7 | SPEAKING PRACTICE

1. Work in small groups. Discuss the comments in section 6 above and compare your personal experiences and challenges with speaking. What are the most common challenges in your group?

2. Brainstorm ways to address the challenges expressed by the group.

8 | TAKING SKILLS FURTHER

Talk with people outside of class who have successfully learned another language. Ask what challenges they faced and how they overcame those difficulties. How do their experiences compare with yours? What strategies did they use that you might like to try? Report your findings in the next class.

For additional listening practice on the topic of the Internet and relationships, go to the *Open Forum* Web site (www.oup.com/elt/openforum) and follow the links.

Topic:	Medical technology
Listening Texts:	Radio interview about cochlear implants; conversation about bio-chip implants
Listening Skill Focus:	Listening for specific information
Speaking Skill Focus:	Expressing limited agreement
Vocabulary:	The endings –*ful* and –*ly*
Pronunciation:	Lengthening vowel sounds before a voiced consonant

1 | INTRODUCING THE TOPIC

Work with a partner. Look at the pictures. Try to answer the questions below. Then compare your answers as a class.

1. What are some benefits technology can offer people who have physical disabilities or medical problems?

2. What are some technological devices that can help people treat medical problems or deal with physical disabilities?

3. Can you name a celebrity who uses medical technology to enhance his or her life?

A Preparing to Listen

You are going to hear a radio interview about a device that can help Deaf people hear. The device, called a cochlear implant, must be surgically inserted in a person's head. Before listening, work with a partner and answer these questions.

1. What kinds of risks do you think might be involved in getting such a device?

2. If you were Deaf would you want to have an electronic device inserted in your head that could help you hear? What if there was a chance that the device would not work?

3. What questions would you want answered before you made a decision about receiving such a device?

B Listening for Main Ideas

Listen to the radio interview. As you listen, number the points in the order they are mentioned. Then compare your answers with a partner.

_____ a. The brain must be trained to recognize sounds transmitted by the cochlear implant.

_____ b. Many Deaf people see cochlear implants as another example that the hearing do not understand or respect Deaf culture.

_____ c. There is no way to predict the benefits of a cochlear implant.

_____ d. Many Deaf people do not consider themselves handicapped and in need of "fixing."

_____ e. A hearing aid is only useful to someone who has some remaining hearing because it makes sounds louder.

C Listening for More Detail

1. Listen to the interview again. Write *T* for true or *F* for false for each statement. Listen again if necessary.

_____ 1. Many people were involved in the development of the cochlear implant.

_____ 2. A cochlear implant works much like a hearing aid.

_____ 3. A cochlear implant will restore hearing to normal.

_____ 4. Some users of cochlear implants can hear music and use the telephone.

_____ 5. Some users are only aware that there is sound in their surrounding area.

_____ 6. If a cochlear implant doesn't work, the person can always use a hearing aid.

_____ 7. A cochlear implant involves invasive surgery.

2. Compare answers with a partner. Correct the false answers to make them true.

D Focus on the Listening Skill: Listening for Specific Information

LISTENING SKILL

When a lot of details are presented in a program or in a lecture, it is sometimes difficult to identify and hear the information that is especially important to you. Practice listening for the specific information that you want to hear, without being distracted by other details.

Read the questions below and identify the information you need to answer the questions. Then listen to the interview again and choose the correct answer for each question.

1. How much can a cochlear implant cost?
   a. between $40,000 and $60,000
   b. around $2,000

2. Does the cochlear implant require a battery?
   a. yes
   b. no

3. How many people around the world have cochlear implants?
   a. around 10,000
   b. around 60,000

4. When did Dr. William House first give a cochlear implant to an American patient?
   a. 1961
   b. 2000

5. How many children in the United States were implanted with cochlear implants?
   a. around 10,000
   b. around 60,000

6. How many adults in the United States have cochlear implants?
   a. around 13,000
   b. around 10,000

E Thinking and Speaking

Discuss these questions with a partner.

1. Do you know anyone who is Deaf or is losing the ability to hear? How do they communicate?

2. Now that you've learned about the cochlear implant, if you were Deaf, would you want one? Explain the reasons for your answer.

3. Do you have any questions about cochlear implants that were not answered in the interview? Where might you find answers to those questions?

3 | VOCABULARY: The adjective ending *–ful* and adverb ending *–ly*

Many adjectives in English have the ending *–ful.* You can often use this ending to create an adjective from a noun. When a word has the ending *–ly,* it is most often an adverb.

1. Look at the following list of common adjectives that have the *–ful* ending.

careful	hopeful
thoughtful	peaceful
painful	thankful
grateful	regretful

2. Read the following list of common adverbs that have the *–ly* ending.

carefully	hopefully
thoughtfully	peacefully
painfully	thankfully
gratefully	regretfully
slowly	eventually
quickly	usually

3. Read the following paragraph. Fill in the missing words using the adjectives and adverbs from exercise 1 and exercise 2.

Deciding whether or not to get a cochlear implant is not easy. The decision requires

(1) _____ thought, and it should be made (2) _____.

The truth is that almost no one who receives the implant is (3) _____

about it. (4) _____, they are (5) _____ for their

newfound ability to hear. However, the adjustment process takes time, and in some

rare cases it can even be (6) _____. Therefore, if you are considering a

cochlear implant for your child, or for yourself, make sure to (7) _____

consider all the information that is available to you. Take your time, and you will

(8) _____ be ready to make an informed choice.

4 | LISTENING PRACTICE

A Preparing to Listen

You are going to hear a conversation about how microchips are being used to store personal information in an interesting way. Before you listen, discuss the following questions with a partner.

1. What kinds of identification cards do you normally carry with you? Do you normally carry medical information with you, for example, information about medicines you are allergic to or any medical conditions you may have?

2. What are the dangers of being in an accident and having no identification or medical information with you?

3. Have you heard the term *microchip* before? What do you think it means?

B Listening for Main Ideas

Read the statements below. Then listen to the conversation. After you listen, check the four main ideas presented by the speakers. (All the ideas are mentioned, but only four of them are main ideas).

_____ a. Implanted microchips can be linked to an ID number and important medical or financial information.

_____ b. Bio-chip implants can be life-saving.

_____ c. Bio-chip implants can make life easier.

_____ d. Privacy and safety are two concerns people have about bio-chip implants.

_____ e. Last year, a doctor received a bio-chip.

_____ f. A European nightclub is using bio-chips.

C Listening for More Detail

Read the questions and answer the ones you can. Then listen to the conversation again and complete your answers. Compare your answers with a partner. Listen again if necessary.

1. What size are the bio-chips, and how are they implanted?

_____

_____

2. What kind of information is stored on the bio-chips?

_____

_____

3. Who could benefit from these implants?

_____

_____

4. How are some European nightclubs using the bio-chips?

_____

_____

5. How expensive are the bio-chip implants?

_____

_____

6. How could the bio-chips be used to invade people's privacy?

_____

_____

7. What is one company going to donate to trauma centers?

_____

_____

D Thinking and Speaking

Work in small groups. Discuss the questions.

1. What concerns would you have about getting a bio-chip implant?

2. Would you let your child get a bio-chip implant? Why or why not?

5 PRONUNCIATION: Lengthening Vowels Before a Voiced Consonant

 FYI Vowels before voiced consonants are held or drawn out longer than vowels before a voiceless consonant. For example, say the words *bad* and *bat*. The vowel sound in *bad* is longer, or stretched out, because it comes before the voiced sound /d/. The vowel sound in *bat* is shorter because it comes before the consonant /t/, which is voiceless.

1. Listen to the following pairs of words. Notice the difference in vowel length.

coat	code
cap	cab
back	bag
tap	tab
safe	save
race	raise

2. Now listen to a word from each pair. Circle the word you hear.

1 coat   code

2 cap   cab

3 back   bag

4 tap   tab

5 safe   save

6 race   raise

3. Listen to these sentences and fill in the blanks with words from the box. Then practice saying the sentences with a partner.

raise   race   code   coat   save   safe

1. The microchip holds a digital _____.

2. The outside of the microchip has a protective _____.

3. This technology could help keep children _____ from kidnappers.

4. Bio-chips could help _____ people's lives.

5. My boss told me to expect a _____.

6. Ellen is training for an important _____.

6 | SPEAKING SKILLS: Expressing Limited Agreement

SPEAKING SKILL

In conversations, especially informal ones, people often use expressions like the ones below to signal that they agree, but not completely.

> OK, but . . .
> I see your point, but . . .
> I agree, but . . .
> On the other hand . . .
> Then again . . .

Listen to the extract from the conversation about bio-chips. Which of the expressions above do the speakers use?

7 | SPEAKING PRACTICE

Work with a partner and discuss the benefits and disadvantages of using bio-chip implants. Do you think the government should require people to have bio-chip implants? Where appropriate, use the expressions above to signal limited agreement.

8 | TAKING SKILLS FURTHER

Watch a TV talk show where two or more people are discussing a topic that interests you. Notice any expressions that the people use to maintain the friendly exchange while expressing limited agreement.

For additional listening practice on the topic of medical technology, go to the *Open Forum* Web site (www.oup.com/elt/openforum) and follow the links.

ABOUT THIS CHAPTER

Topic:	The Nobel Prizes
Listening Texts:	Student presentation on the Nobel Prizes; conversation about Kim Dae Jung
Listening Skill Focus:	Identifying restatements and explanations
Speaking Skill Focus:	Checking for understanding
Vocabulary:	Nouns for professions with –*ist*
Pronunciation:	The vowel sounds /ɪ/ and /iy/

1 INTRODUCING THE TOPIC

Almost every year, a person or an organization wins the Nobel Peace Prize. Take the following quiz to find out how much you know about past winners. The answers are at the bottom of the page.

NOBEL PEACE PRIZE WINNERS

Try to match each person or organization with the correct description.

_____1. Wangari Maathai, Kenya (2004)

_____2. Doctors without Borders, Belgium (1999)

_____3. Jimmy Carter, USA (2002)

_____4. International Atomic Energy Agency (2005)

_____5. Shirin Ebadi, Iran (2003)

a. Won the Nobel Peace Prize for their work internationally dedicated to improving conditions for people in emergencies

b. Won the Nobel Prize for his work towards resolving international conflicts

c. Won the Nobel Prize for her Greenbelt Movement, an environmental agency

d. Won the Nobel Peace Prize for her human rights work, especially for women and children

e. Won the Nobel Peace Prize for their work to make sure nuclear energy is safely used for peaceful purposes

Answers: 1. c; 2. a; 3. b; 4. e; 5. d

2 | LISTENING PRACTICE

A Preparing to Listen

You are going to hear a student presentation about the history of the Nobel Prize. Before you listen, read the list of topics below. Check the topics you think the students will discuss in the presentation.

_____ a. Who the Nobel Prize is named for

_____ b. How often the prizes are awarded

_____ c. Where the prizes are awarded

_____ d. The names of all the prize winners

_____ e. The categories for Nobel Prizes

_____ f. Other prizes similar to the Nobel Prizes

B Listening for Main Ideas

Listen to the student presentation. Then choose the correct answer for each question.

1. Why did Alfred Nobel establish the Nobel Prizes?
   a. To recognize people who work to improve the world
   b. To celebrate his invention of dynamite
   c. To end controversy in the field of physics

2. Which of the statements is not true?
   a. Many winners don't keep the prize money.
   b. Candidates usually know they've been nominated.
   c. The prize given in the field of economics is not really a Nobel Prize.

3. Why do some people believe that Rosalind Franklin's name should have been added to those of Watson, Crick, and Wilkins for the 1962 Nobel Prize in Physiology and Medicine?
   a. She cannot receive the award posthumously.
   b. Without looking at her work, Watson, Crick, and Wilkins would not have discovered the structure of the DNA double helix.
   c. She alone was responsible for identifying the DNA double helix.

C Focus on the Listening Skill: Identifying Restatements and Explanations

> **LISTENING SKILL**
>
> Speakers will often restate what they just said in different words in order to explain what they mean. When they restate something using different words, it helps to make the meaning clearer for their listeners. Here are some expressions that show that a speaker is going to say something again in a new way.

That is, . . .	What I mean is . . .
In other words, . . .	What I'm trying to say is . . .

Listen and read an extract from the presentation. Write the expressions that the speakers use to restate what they have said in a new way.

In his last will, Alfred Nobel left more than 90% of his estate—(1) _____, almost his entire fortune—to establish the Nobel Prizes for "those who, during the preceding year shall have conferred the greatest benefit on mankind." (2) _____, he wanted to give awards each year to people who had done something important and good for the world. The awards are given in the following disciplines: medicine, chemistry, literature, peace, and physics. There's also a prize for economics that carries Nobel's name, but it was established much later and is not truly a Nobel Prize. (3) _____, it was not one of the prizes that Alfred Nobel himself founded.

Thank you, Robbie. The process for determining the recipients begins more than one year before the awards are actually handed out. (4) _____, a committee begins to think about possible candidates each fall, and then the prizes are finally handed out to the winners in the winter of the following year. There are sometimes as many as 250 candidates for a particular award; however, the nominees have no idea that they have been nominated, and they are often surprised to find out that they have won. Each winner receives a certificate and a medal. Each winner is awarded a little over 1 million dollars, as well. Winners often donate the money to projects or causes that are important to them, but this isn't required. (5) _____, they can keep the money if they want to. Another interesting fact is that it's not customary to make awards posthumously. (6) _____, Nobel Prize winners must still be living at the time that the awards are announced.

D Thinking and Speaking

Discuss the following questions in small groups.

1. Have there been any Nobel Prize winners from your country? What did they win for?

2. Are there any people you would personally nominate to receive a Nobel Prize? Why do you think they deserve to win the award?

3. Who are some of your heroes? What have they done and how have they affected you?

3 VOCABULARY: Nouns for Professions with –ist

 Words ending in *–ist* often refer to a person who works in a certain profession. For example, *–ist* is used to say that someone who works in the field of science is a *scientist*.

1. Try to match each profession with the correct definition. Then compare answers with a partner.

_a_	1. activist	a. A person who fights for social causes or political change
____	2. scientist	b. A person who studies ancient peoples and their cultures
____	3. cartoonist	c. A person who fills drug prescriptions and works in a pharmacy
____	4. receptionist	d. A person who has a great deal of knowledge of one or more of the sciences
____	5. archaeologist	e. A person who takes care of hands and fingernails by performing manicures
____	6. therapist	g. A person who performs therapy to help people with certain problems
____	7. pharmacist	h. A person who draws illustrations and cartoons
____	8. manicurist	i. A person who works in an office receiving phone calls and doing paperwork

2. **Work in pairs or small groups. Look at the list below. What do you think these people do? Do you know any more jobs that end in *–ist*?**

biologist	optometrist
chemist	zoologist
geologist	cyclist
arborist	

3. **Discuss the following questions with a partner.**

   1. Do any of the professions in exercise 1 and 2 appeal to you? If so, which ones?

   2. How much training is involved for the careers you're interested in?

   3. What do you think are the most popular career fields right now?

4 LISTENING PRACTICE

A Preparing to Listen

Look at the photograph below. What do you think is happening in the picture? Discuss your answers as a class.

B Listening for Main Ideas

Listen to a college lecture. As you listen, choose the correct answer to each question.

1. Who was the Nobel Peace Prize winner in 2000?
   a. Octavio Paz
   b. Desmond Tuto
   c. Kim Dae-Jung

2. What did he win it for?
   a. His work at Harvard
   b. His Sunshine Policy
   c. His economic reforms

C Listening for More Detail

Read the questions and answer the ones you that you can. Then listen to the lecture again and answer the rest of the questions. Compare answers with a partner. Listen again if necessary.

1. Where was Kim Dae-Jung born?

_____

_____

2. Why were there several attempts on his life?

_____

_____

3. Where did Kim spend time in the US?

_____

_____

4. What happened when he returned to Korea?

_____

_____

5. What happened under Kim's Sunshine Policy?

_____

_____

6. Why is it called the Sunshine Policy?

_____

_____

D Working Out Unknown Vocabulary

Listen to the extracts from the lecture. Listen for the words and expressions in italics. Choose the correct meaning for each word or expression. Then compare answers with a partner.

1. *A bunch of* probably means _____.
   a. many
   b. a few

2. *On the verge of* probably means _____.
   a. finished
   b. almost, close to

3. *Reconciliation* probably means _____.
   a. becoming enemies
   b. becoming friendly

4. *Resolve* probably means _____.
   a. find a solution to a problem or conflict
   b. fight aggressively

E Thinking and Speaking

Discuss the following questions in pairs.

1. It takes courage to stand up to a government or society and not give up working towards a goal. Are you this kind of person? How do you know?

2. Many countries require young people to serve in the military. What do you think of this?

5 PRONUNCIATION: The vowel sounds /ɪ/ and /iy/

Many people have trouble saying and hearing the difference between the vowel sound /ɪ/ as in *it* and vowel sound /iy/ as in *eat*. To say /ɪ/, relax your lips and keep your tongue low in your mouth. Your tongue does not move. To say /iy/, stretch your lips and move the center of your tongue up to the roof of your mouth.

1. Listen to these pairs of words. Notice the difference between the vowel sounds in each pair.

/ɪ/	/iy/
it	eat
live	leave
chip	cheap
ship	sheep
fit	feet

2. Listen to these sentences. Circle the word you hear.

	/ɪ/	/iy/
1.	it	eat
2.	live	leave
3.	chip	cheap
4.	ship	sheep
5.	fit	feet

3. Listen to the sentences. Circle the vowel sound you hear in the underlined word.

1. Who's the <u>winner</u>? /ɪ/ /iy/

2. His name is <u>Kim</u>. /ɪ/ /iy/

3. He's from <u>Korea</u>. /ɪ/ /iy/

4. He won the <u>Peace</u> Prize. /ɪ/ /iy/

5. Several <u>people</u> were nominated. /ɪ/ /iy/

6. The fable is about the sun and the <u>wind</u>. /ɪ/ /iy/

4. Work with a partner and practice saying the sentences above.

6 SPEAKING SKILLS: Checking for Understanding

SPEAKING SKILL

If you aren't sure if you understood what someone said, you can ask for an explanation or rephrase what the speaker said in order to verify meaning.

Asking for an Explanation	Rephrasing
Do you mean . . . ?	So you mean . . .
I'm not sure I understand.	Okay, so you're saying . . .
What do you mean by . . . ?	Your saying that . . .
Did you say . . . ?	You said that . . .

1. Listen to four extracts from the recording. Write the expressions that the speakers use to check for comprehension.

1. _____

2. _____

3. _____

4. _____

2. Listen to a short interview and answer the questions.

1. What are the people talking about?

_____

_____

2. What is Emily's opinion?

_____

_____

 3. Listen to the interview again. Which expressions does the interviewer use to check for understanding?

7 SPEAKING PRACTICE

1. Work in pairs. Read the list of proverbs below. Each one is taken from one of Aesop's Fables. Choose three or four of the proverbs and discuss the lessons they teach.

- Don't count your chickens before they've hatched.
- Do unto others as you would have them do unto you.
- You can't please everyone.
- Birds of a feather flock together.
- United we stand, divided we fall.
- Misery loves company.
- Look before you leap.
- Familiarity breeds contempt.
- Honesty is the best policy.

2. Do you remember any fables that you were taught as a child? What lessons do they teach?

8 TAKING SKILLS FURTHER

Listen to interviews on TV or the radio. Listen for the expressions that the speakers use to check for understanding. Compare your findings in the next class.

www For additional listening practice on the topic of the Nobel Prizes, go to the *Open Forum* Web site (www.oup.com/elt/openforum) and follow the links.

ABOUT THIS CHAPTER

Topic:	Extreme weather conditions
Listening Texts:	Lecture about desertification; interview about hurricanes
Listening Skill Focus:	Key phrases to introduce an example
Speaking Skill Focus:	Using repairs
Vocabulary:	Words related to land use
Pronunciation:	*Can* vs. *can't*

1 INTRODUCING THE TOPIC

1. Look at the quiz from a science class. Work with a partner and try to answer the questions. (The answers are at the bottom of the page.)

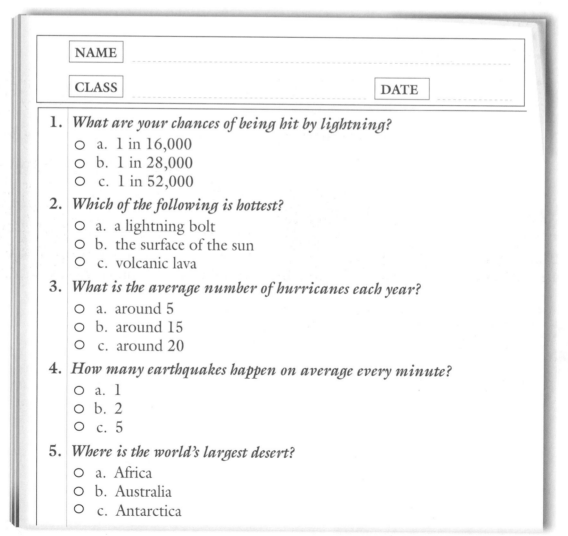

NAME _____

CLASS _____   DATE _____

1. *What are your chances of being hit by lightning?*
   - a. 1 in 16,000
   - b. 1 in 28,000
   - c. 1 in 52,000

2. *Which of the following is hottest?*
   - a. a lightning bolt
   - b. the surface of the sun
   - c. volcanic lava

3. *What is the average number of hurricanes each year?*
   - a. around 5
   - b. around 15
   - c. around 20

4. *How many earthquakes happen on average every minute?*
   - a. 1
   - b. 2
   - c. 5

5. *Where is the world's largest desert?*
   - a. Africa
   - b. Australia
   - c. Antarctica

Answers: 1. b, 2. a, 3. c, 4. b, 5. c

2. Look at the following list of natural phenomena. Check the ones that happen where you live? Discuss your choices in pairs.

_____ earthquakes   _____ tsunamis   _____ hurricanes   _____ drought

_____ tornadoes   _____ volcanoes   _____ typhoons   _____ floods

3. Have you ever experienced a natural disaster? What happened? What did you do?

2 | LISTENING PRACTICE

A Preparing to Listen

1. You are going to hear a lecture about the problem of desertification. Look at the pictures below. Then discuss the questions.

1. What do you think desertification means?
2. What do you think causes desertification?

B Listening for Main Ideas

Listen to the lecture. Then check your answers to the questions above. Did you answer them correctly?

C Listening for More Detail

Read through the questions and answer the ones you can. Then listen
to the lecture again and complete your answers as you listen. Compare
answers with a partner.

1. Who is giving this lecture? _____

_____

2. How many countries have areas that suffer from desertification?_____

_____

3. How long does it take for desertification to take place _____

_____

4. How can cutting down trees cause desertification? _____

_____

5. How are livestock and cattle affected by desertification? _____

_____

6. According to the lecture, by 2020, how many people will be forced to leave their
homes because of desertification?_____

_____

7. What are some of the places where desertification is happening? _____

_____

D Focus on the Listening Skill: Key Phrases to Introduce an Example

LISTENING SKILL

Listening for examples will help you to understand a speaker's
meaning. Speakers often use the following key phrases to introduce
an example to support their ideas.

> For example, . . .
> For instance, . . .
> Let me give you an example.
> An example of this is . . .

Point	Examples
1. Many factors affect desertification.	
2. Desertification can cause many other problems.	
3. Overgrazing causes desertification.	
4. Governments are doing many things to stop desertification.	
5. There are many ways that you can learn more about desertification.	

E Thinking and Speaking

Discuss the questions with a partner.

1. What are some of the consequences if desertification continues?

2. How important is farming where you live? Are any crops grown there?

3. What would happen if the land farmers use became unusable?

3 VOCABULARY: Words Related to Land Use

1. Read the sentences below paying attention to the words in bold. Then write your own definition of the words in bold.

   1. My country had almost no rain for three years. Many people suffered greatly during this long **drought.**

      Drought probably means: _____

   2. When the rain finally started to fall, the land couldn't absorb it all so there was a **deluge** that washed away everything in its path.

      Deluge probably means: _____

   3. Our poor cows! We couldn't feed our **livestock** because all the grass had died.

      Livestock probably means: _____

   4. All the **crops** died. There was no corn, no rice, no vegetables or fruit.

      Crops probably means: _____

   5. After several years, the top layer of land finally became rich again. Once again, we could plant in the **topsoil**.

      Topsoil probably means: _____

2. Read the passage from a report. Fill in the blanks with the words in bold from exercise 1. Compare your answers with a partner.

The Dust Bowl

In central North America during the Dust Bowl, a period of time in the 1930s marked by dust storms and other severe weather conditions, many people were forced out of their homes due to economic necessity. Years of over planting wheat, combined with a (1) _____ resulted in dried up areas of grasslands. The wind picked up dirt creating clouds that blew for miles, sometimes turning "day into night." Formerly good (2) _____ was ripped up and blown across the plains, leaving the land useless for growing wheat and other vegetation. As a result, farmers could no longer feed their (3) _____. After this long period of dry weather, rains and storms came, resulting in a severe (4) _____. Farmers left their homes and went in search of work picking (5) _____ in other states. Some estimates say that roughly 300,000 people from Oklahoma had to leave their homes.

4 LISTENING PRACTICE

A Preparing to Listen

You are going to hear an interview with a hurricane hunter. Work with a partner. Discuss possible answers to the following questions.

1. What is a hurricane hunter?
2. How do hurricanes form?
3. What can we learn from studying hurricanes?

B Listening for Main Ideas

🎧 Listen to the interview. Then note the three main topics presented by the hurricane hunter.

1. _____

2. _____

3. _____

C Listening for More Details

🎧 Listen again. Write *T* for true and *F* for false for each statement. Correct the false statements. Then compare answers with a partner.

_____ 1. A tropical storm in the Northwest Pacific is called a typhoon.

_____ 2. Heat is released when warm air rises, cools, and condenses.

_____ 3. Hurricanes rotate east to west north of the equator.

_____ 4. A category 5 hurricane is very strong.

_____ 5. Hurricane hunters look for ways to stop the destructive power of hurricanes.

_____ 6. Hurricane hunters fly quickly into the eye of the storm.

_____ 7. They collect data which adds to our understanding of the nature of hurricanes.

_____ 8. Hurricane hunters enter and re-enter the storm one or two times during a mission.

D Working Out Unknown Vocabulary

🎧 Listen to four extracts from the interview. Listen for the words in italics. Then choose the correct meaning for each word.

1. *Condense* probably means _____.
   a. change from gas to liquid
   b. get windy

2. *Rotate* probably means _____.
   a. turn on a center point
   b. travel

3. *Landfall* probably means _____.
   a. move off land
   b. arrive on land

4. *Evacuate* probably means _____.
   a. leave an area to be safe
   b. remain in the same place and be careful

E Thinking and Speaking

Discuss these questions in pairs.

1. Do you live in an area where hurricanes hit? What should you do to be prepared?

2. If you had the opportunity to fly into the eye of a hurricane, would you do it? Explain your answer.

5 PRONUNCIATION: *Can* vs. *Can't*

 Many people have trouble hearing the difference between the words *can* and *can't*. The difference is not the final /t/ in *can't*, but it's the vowel. When we speak quickly, the vowel in *can* is reduced to /ə/. The vowel in *can't* is pronounced /ae/, as in *sad*, or *hat*.

1. Listen to the extracts from the interview. Circle the word you hear.

   1.   can   can't

   2.   can   can't

   3.   can   can't

   4.   can   can't

   5.   can   can't

2. Read and listen to the paragraph written by a high school student. Fill in the blanks with *can* or *can't*.

This semester we (1) _____ take two electives along with

Earth Science, Math, and English, but we (2) _____ take two

art classes, or two P.E. courses. This is okay because next year when I'm a senior,

I (3) _____ take whatever I need to finish my requirements for

graduation. As seniors, we (4) _____ also go off campus for

lunch; something the younger students (5) _____ do, and we

(6) _____ start taking college classes if we have the time. Before

graduation, our class is going on a senior a trip, but I (7) _____ go

because I'll have to work to save money so I (8) _____ go to college.

3. Complete the sentences. Then read your sentences to a partner.

1. I can _____, but I can't _____.

2. My best friend can _____, but he/she can't

   _____.

3. I can _____ pretty well.

4. I can't _____ well at all.

5. My teacher can _____.

6. My classmates can't _____.

6 SPEAKING SKILLS: Using Repairs

SPEAKING SKILL

Speakers often make mistakes when they talk. For instance, they
might make false starts, use the wrong word, or mispronounce
words. This is a normal part of conversation. If you make a mistake
when you are speaking, try to repair the mistake by repeating,
rephrasing, or explaining what you were trying to say.

1. Listen to extracts from the report. In each extract the speaker makes a
   mistake. What does the speaker do to repair the mistake? Circle the correct
   answer.

   1. repeat   rephrase   explain

   2. repeat   rephrase   explain

   3. repeat   rephrase   explain

   4. repeat   rephrase   explain

   5. repeat   rephrase   explain

1. Work in groups of three. Students 1 and 2: Discuss one of the questions in the chart below. Use repairs to keep the conversation going. Student 3: Listen for repairs. Make a mark every time each speaker uses a repair. Take turns discussing and counting.

Topic	Student 1	Student 2
What should you keep in an emergency kit at home?	_____ repeat _____ rephrase _____ explain	_____ repeat _____ rephrase _____ explain
What should you do in case of a disaster, like a hurricane, an earthquake, or a flood?	_____ repeat _____ rephrase _____ explain	_____ repeat _____ rephrase _____ explain
Do you know of any jobs that are more dangerous than hurricane hunting? What are they?	_____ repeat _____ rephrase _____ explain	_____ repeat _____ rephrase _____ explain

2. Which type of repair did the speakers use most often? Compare your results as a class.

8 | **TAKING SKILLS FURTHER**

Outside of class, pay attention to conversations between people. Notice when they make false starts, use the wrong word, or mispronounce a word. How do they repair these mistakes? Compare your findings in the next class.

For additional listening practice on the topic of extreme weather, go to the *Open Forum* Web site (www.oup.com/elt/openforum) and follow the links.

ABOUT THIS CHAPTER

Topic:	Amazing animal abilities
Listening Texts:	Radio interview about animal senses; Television program about bower birds
Listening Skill Focus:	Key phrases to introduce important facts
Speaking Skill Focus:	Using Imprecision
Vocabulary:	Multi-word verbs
Pronunciation:	Contractions with nouns

1 INTRODUCING THE TOPIC

Work with a partner. Read the quiz from a Website and discuss possible answers to the questions. (The answers are at the bottom of the page.)

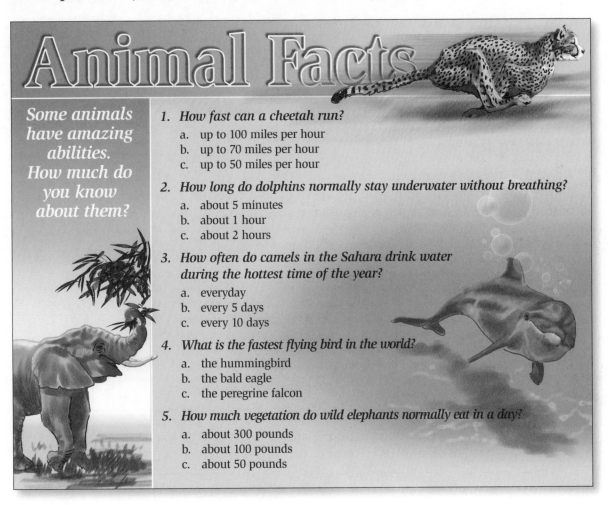

Animal Facts

Some animals have amazing abilities. How much do you know about them?

1. **How fast can a cheetah run?**
   a. up to 100 miles per hour
   b. up to 70 miles per hour
   c. up to 50 miles per hour

2. **How long do dolphins normally stay underwater without breathing?**
   a. about 5 minutes
   b. about 1 hour
   c. about 2 hours

3. **How often do camels in the Sahara drink water during the hottest time of the year?**
   a. everyday
   b. every 5 days
   c. every 10 days

4. **What is the fastest flying bird in the world?**
   a. the hummingbird
   b. the bald eagle
   c. the peregrine falcon

5. **How much vegetation do wild elephants normally eat in a day?**
   a. about 300 pounds
   b. about 100 pounds
   c. about 50 pounds

Answers: 1. b, 2. a, 3. b, 4. c, 5. a

2 LISTENING PRACTICE

A Preparing to Listen

You are going to hear a radio program about how certain animals are able to sense approaching earthquakes. Before you listen, work with a partner and discuss possible answers to the following questions.

1. How can animals sense that an earthquake is approaching?
2. What do you think an animal will do if it senses an approaching earthquake?
3. How can this ability help humans?

B Listening for Main Ideas

Listen to the radio program. Check the three main ideas that are discussed. (All the ideas are mentioned.)

_____ a. Animals can smell, hear and feel things that humans don't or can't.

_____ b. Some animals can sense earthquakes before they happen.

_____ c. Elephants are not good predictors of earthquakes.

_____ d. Scientists around the world are paying more attention to animal behavior because they believe animals can save lives by making use of their extraordinary senses.

C Listening for More Detail

Read the questions and answer the ones that you can. Then listen to the conversation again and answer the rest of the questions. Compare answers with a partner. Listen again if necessary.

1. What do some pets do before an earthquake? _____

_____

_____

2. What is infrasound and who can pick it up? _____

_____

_____

3. How long ago were animal premonitions of earthquakes documented?

_____

4. How do elephants know that there are other elephants miles away?

_____

_____

5. What are two ways we make use of dogs' sense of smell? _____

_____

6. Where do seismologists in China get information about unusual animal behavior?

_____

_____

D Focus on the Listening Skill: Key Phrases to Introduce Important Facts

LISTENING SKILL

Speakers often use key phrases to introduce important details and to establish certain points as facts. Pay attention to what follows these key phrases because it is probably important information.

In fact . . .
It is widely accepted that . . .
It is widely known that . . .
Experts/scientists /reports/claim that . . .

Listen to extracts from the program and complete the sentences with the key phrase you hear.

1. Well, _____ animals possess a finer sense of smell than we do.

2. _____, manufacturers have taken advantage of these different abilities to hear sounds.

3. _____ there are some other senses that we don't yet understand.

4. _____, my own dog senses storms when they are pretty far off.

E Thinking and Speaking

Discuss these questions in pairs or small groups.

1. What unusual animal behavior have you seen or heard about?

2. What are some ways that animals' senses are being used to serve people?

3. Do you think it is ethical to use animals to serve humans? Why or why not?

3 VOCABULARY: Multi-Word Verbs

1. Each sentence below contains a multi-word verb in bold. Read each sentence. Then match each multi-word verb with its definition. Compare your answers in small groups.

    1. We **were used to** earthquakes because they happened often.

    2. Scientists are **paying attention to** animals' behavior.

    3. In China they're **counting on** animal behavior to **tip** them **off** in advance.

    4. Some people in the US **are open to** the idea.

    5. Dogs, some birds, and elephants can **pick up** infrasound and or vibrations.

Multi-Word Verb	Definition
_____ 1. be used to	a. recognize, sense
_____ 2. pay attention to	b. observe, watch closely
_____ 3. count on	c. be familiar with
_____ 4. tip off	d. be willing to consider
_____ 5. be open to	e. rely on, depend on
_____ 6. pick up	f. reveal information

2. Fill in each blank with the correct form of one of the multi-word verbs above. Then compare answers in small groups.

    1. My boss is not very good at _____ on subtle hints.

    2. Nobody _____ the flight attendants' announcement about emergency exits. Everyone's heard it a million times.

    3. I think someone already _____ Jim about the surprise party because he didn't look very surprised.

    4. Earthquakes happen pretty often in California, so Californians

    _____ them.

    5. Some Americans _____ Eastern medicine and natural ways of healing. They are willing to try these old Eastern methods.

    6. You are important to this mission! We _____ your participation.

3. Complete the following sentences. Discuss your answers with a partner.

    1. I am still not used to _____.

    2. To resolve differences, it's important to be open to _____.

    3. You can always count on _____.

LISTENING PRACTICE

A Preparing to Listen

Look at these photographs of structures built by birds. Then discuss the
questions below with a partner.

1. How would you describe each structure?

2. What do you think is the purpose of these structures?

B Listening for Main Ideas

Listen to a program about bower birds. As you listen, note your answers to the
following questions:

1. What do bower birds do that the speaker finds so special? _____

_____

_____

2. How do bower birds learn to build nests? _____

_____

_____

3. What do birds do to other birds' bowers? _____

_____

_____

4. Note some words that the speakers use to describe the birds. _____

_____

_____

C Listening for More Detail

🎧 Read the questions and answer the ones you can. Then listen to the program again and answer the remaining questions. Compare answers with a partner. Listen again if necessary.

1. What are some examples of behavior birds use to attract a mate? _____

   _____

2. What do bower birds do to help raise the young or chicks? _____

   _____

3. How are maypole bowers constructed? _____

   _____

4. List some objects bower birds might use to decorate their structures. _____

   _____

5. How do experts think the birds learn to build these structures? And how long does it

   take to develop this skill? _____

   _____

6. Why does the speaker describe bower birds as thieves? _____

   _____

D Working Out Unknown Vocabulary

🎧 Listen to the extracts from the program. Listen for the words and expressions in italics. Choose the correct meaning for each word or expression.

1. *Courtship* probably means _____.
   a. behavior to attract a mate
   b. a structure where birds mate

2. *Fluff up* probably means _____.
   a. ruffle or make puffy
   b. wash

3. *Show off* probably means _____.
   a. behave conspicuously in order to be seen
   b. escape or run away

4. *Erected* probably means _____.
   a. destroyed
   b. built, constructed

E Thinking and Speaking

Discuss the questions in small groups.

   1. What about the birds' behavior is surprising? Why?

   2. How do some other animals attract mates?

5 PRONUNCIATION: Contractions with Nouns

In spoken English, auxiliary verbs such as *are*, *will*, and *had* often contract with a noun. For example, speakers may say the sentence, "He had already left" as "*He'd* already left." Or they might pronounce the sentence, "My son will be there" as "My *son'll* be there."

1. Listen to the sentences and notice how the words in italics are contracted.

   1. These *bowers are* erected and decorated to attract mates.

   2. One *birds had* placed a large black mushroom in the center of the lawn.

   3. The *birds will* use almost anything . . .

   4. Birds were carrying off things *kids had* left out.

2. Listen to the sentences and write the full form of the contractions you hear.

   1. This _____ been sabotaged by a rival bird.

   2. The _____ been moved and tossed here and there.

   3. The _____ be annoyed when he sees the damage.

   4. What do you think the _____ do?

3. Practice saying the sentences to a partner. Use contractions instead of the full forms you wrote.

6 SPEAKING SKILLS: Using Imprecision

SPEAKING SKILL

When you are not sure that you have chosen the right word to describe
something, or you want to seem less direct, use expressions such as the
ones below to express imprecision.

Expression	Example
about / around / approximately	We'll be there in about an hour.
it's as though / it's as if / it's like	It's as though he was scared.
kind of / sort of	It's sort of cold in here.
or something (like that)	I'll bring a desert or something.

1. Read a description of bower birds' behavior. Then listen to what was actually
   said in the program. How is the spoken version different from what is written
   below? What effect do the differences have?

   You've probably seen nature programs showing how some birds behave in
   strange ways to attract a mate. Sometimes they do a little dance, or fluff up
   their feathers. They're showing off to attract a mate. Bower birds use physical
   displays too, but what is really amazing are the structures, or bowers,
   that they build.

2. Listen to an extract from the program on animal senses. Fill in the missing words.

   It's (1) _____ strange. All the animals, three cats and the dog,

   do the same thing at (2) _____ the same time. They gather

   together and won't stand up—they (3) _____ crouch down or

   lie flat in the center of the room. They'll stay there for (4) _____

   two minutes. If my husband and I are in another room, they'll come into the room

   where we are. It's (5) _____ they want to stick together

   (6) _____. I've definitely seen them do that just before an

   earthquake, but we've also noticed it other times when we didn't feel any tremors.

   Oddly enough, though, we would sometimes hear on the news the next day that

   there had been a mild quake or some tremors. We would think, it's

   (7) _____ they knew the earthquake was coming!

7 | SPEAKING PRACTICE

1. Choose one of the people, places, or things in the list and write a short description of it. Try to give several details..

   A place you enjoy visiting
   Your first job
   Your first English teacher
   Your best friend
   A book or movie you enjoyed

2. Work with a partner. Student A: Look over your written description. Then, without reading, describe the person, place, or thing to Student B. Try to use some of the expressions from Section 6. Student B: Listen to Student A's description. Can you imagine what he or she is describing? Take turns describing and listening.

8 | TAKING SKILLS FURTHER

Outside of class, ask some native speakers to describe their hometown to you. As you listen, notice if they use any of the expressions in Section 6. Discuss your findings in the next class.

For additional listening practice on the topic of animal abilities, go to the *Open Forum* Web site (www.oup.com/elt/openforum) and follow the links.

Topics:	Optimism and pessimism; visualization
Listening Texts:	College lecture on optimism and pessimism, conversation about visualization
Listening Skill Focus:	Signaling comparison and contrast
Speaking Skill Focus:	Expressing opinions
Vocabulary:	Verbs starting with *out–*
Pronunciation:	Silent *h* in pronouns

1 | INTRODUCING THE TOPIC

1. Work with a partner. Look at the pictures. What are the people doing?
    What are some possible reasons for these practices? What are some
    possible benefits?

2. Compare and discuss your answers with a partner.

A Preparing to Listen

1. Look at the photograph. Some people would say the glass is half empty. Others might say it's half full. How would you describe it?

2. You are going to hear a college lecture about optimism and pessimism. Before you listen, work with a partner and try to answer the questions.

   1. What is optimism? How can you tell that someone is an optimist?

   2. What is pessimism? How can you tell that someone is a pessimist?

B Listening for Main Ideas

Listen and check your answers to the questions above. Were your answers correct?

C Listening for More Details

Listen to the lecture again. Choose the correct answer to complete each statement. Then compare answers with a partner. Listen again if necessary.

1. The expression *seeing the glass half full* refers to _____.
   a. optimists
   b. pessimists

2. _____ may determine if a person is an optimist or a pessimist.
   a. Education
   b. Genetics

3. _____ recover more quickly from surgery and have fewer complications.
   a. optimists
   b. pessimists

4. _____ overcome obstacles more easily.
   a. optimists
   b. pessimists

5. _____ find it easier to admit how bad a situation is.
   a. optimists
   b. pessimists

6. If you are a pessimist by nature, you _____ change.
   a. can
   b. can't

D Focus on the Listening Skill: Signaling Comparison and Contrast

> **LISTENING SKILL**
>
> Speakers often use certain expressions to show contrast, how something is different from something else. They also use certain expressions to show comparison, how something is similar to something else.

1. **Listen to extracts from the lecture. Decide whether the expression in italics is indicating a contrast or a comparison. Discuss your answers in pairs.**

   1. Optimism is typically defined as the attitude of believing in and expecting positive results, *while* pessimism is the tendency to believe in negative outcomes.

      While indicates contrast / comparison.

   2. Pessimists tend not to take very good care of themselves in general. *On the other hand*, people who were rated optimistic tend to be healthier.

      On the other hand indicates contrast / comparison.

   3. Adults who were rated optimistic recovered more quickly in the short and long run after operations and had fewer hospital readmissions than pessimists. *Similarly*, young students who were rated optimistic consistently were more successful in surmounting obstacles in school.

      Similarly indicates contrast / comparison.

   4. Young students who were rated optimistic consistently were more successful in surmounting obstacles in school. And when suffering a set back, they came back and overcame the difficulty successfully. *In contrast*, pessimists did worse when attempting a retry.

      In contrast indicates contrast / comparison.

   5. At a glance, it might seem as if that were true, *however*, the research shows that true optimists are not in denial.

      However indicates contrast / comparison.

   6. If you catch yourself having negative thoughts about yourself, *like* many pessimists do, stop and think about what's going right in your life.

      Like indicates contrast / comparison.

   7. *Unlike* optimists, many pessimists give up on a project when it becomes too difficult.

      Unlike indicates contrast / comparison.

2. Finish the sentences below with an appropriate ending. Then practice saying your sentences with a partner.

1. While I believe psychology is interesting, I _____.

2. Unlike my father, I _____.

3. I like biology; on the other hand, _____.

4. To me, studying English is similar to _____.

5. I do well in science classes; however, _____.

6. Much like my mother, I _____.

E Thinking and Speaking

Discuss the questions with a partner.

1. Would you say that you are a pessimist or an optimist? Why?

2. How can someone change from being a pessimist to being an optimist, or vice versa?

4. Is it possible to be neither an optimist nor a pessimist? Explain your answer.

3 VOCABULARY: Verbs Starting with *Out*–

 The prefix *out*– before a verb usually means to do better, exceed, or surpass someone or something else. For instance, in the following sentence *outlast* means *last longer than:* "I hope this new car outlasts my previous one."

1. Read the list of verbs with *out*– below. Match each word with it's definition.

_____ 1. Outdistance	a. to be in a higher class
_____ 2. Outdo	b. to perform better in a sport
_____ 3. Outsell	c. to go farther
_____ 4. Outclass	d. to perform better, to do better
_____ 5. Outplay	e. to sell more

2. What do you think these words mean. Discuss your answers with a partner.

   1. Outrun
   2. Outperform
   3. Outsmart
   4. Outfox

3. Check your answers in a dictionary.

4 | LISTENING PRACTICE

A Preparing to Listen

1. Look at the following list of ways that an athlete can prepare for competition and add any other practices that you can think of.

   • Lift weights regularly.
   • Eat healthy foods.
   • Sleep well the night before the competition.
   • Study the strategies of your opponent.
   • Run or jog regularly.
   • Practice everyday.
   • _____
   • _____
   • _____

2. Think of a sport that you enjoy watching or participating in. Circle the three practices above that you think are most important to prepare for this sport.

3. Compare your choices with a partner. Then answer the following questions.

　　1. What is more important when preparing for athletic competition: physical preparation or mental preparation? Explain your answer.

　　2. How can an athlete prepare mentally for a competition?

B Listening for Main Ideas

Listen to the conversation between two teammates. Then answer the questions.

　　1. Why is Jeremy doing so well in track? _____

　　_____

　　2. What does Cesar help him do? _____

　　_____

C Listening for More Detail

Listen to the conversation again. As you listen, write *T* for true and *F* for false for each statement. Compare answers with a partner. Correct the false statements to make them true. Listen again if necessary.

　　_____ 1. Jeremy has improved.

　　_____ 2. Jeremy is doing more exercises.

　　_____ 3. Olympic athletes use visualization coaches.

　　_____ 4. A visualization coach helps a person imagine doing something well before he/she actually does it.

　　_____ 5. Jeremy meets his coach every day.

　　_____ 6. Cesar tells Jeremy to think about what to do if he has a problem while on the track.

　　_____ 7. Jeremy doesn't need to work out or train anymore.

　　_____ 8. Thinking about what you're going to do helps you when you actually do it.

　　_____ 9. Jeremy is going to give Rob his coach's number.

D Working Out Unknown Vocabulary

Listen to the extracts from the conversation. Listen for the words and expressions in italics. Choose the correct meaning for each word or expression.

1. *Scholarship* probably means _____.
   a. money given to a student to attend college
   b. money paid by a student to attend college

2. *Mark* probably means _____.
   a. starting line
   b. track

3. *Fan* probably means _____.
   a. a person who trains with a team or athlete
   b. a person who supports a team or athlete

4. *Pave the way* probably means _____.
   a. to dream
   b. to make something easier

E Thinking and Speaking

Discuss the questions with a partner. Then compare and discuss answers as a class.

1. Do you play a sport? How do you train?

2. How do you prepare mentally for the challenges that you face at work, at school, or at home?

3. Do you think sports visualization works? Explain your answer?

4. How do you think sports visualization might be used in other areas of life, other than sports?

5 | PRONUNCIATION: Silent *h* in Pronouns

When people speak quickly, the *h* in the pronouns *he*, *him*, *his*, *her*, and *hers* is often not pronounced. For example, when someone says, "Does he?" quickly, it sounds like, "Duzee?" Note: If the pronoun begins a sentence, the *h* is always pronounced.

1. **Listen to extracts from the conversation. Write the missing words.**

   1. _____ _____ tells me to try and visualize myself doing it, too.

   2. He'll play fan noises like we're in a real stadium when I'm doing my training _____ _____.

   3. It's _____ _____ wants me to get used to noise distractions and visualize myself winning in spite of them.

   4. So, _____ _____ do anything else?

   5. Usually, I _____ _____ a couple hours a week.

2. **Listen to five questions. Choose the answer that best fits each question.**

   1. a. My name is Sheila.
      b. Her name is Janet.

   2. a. His name is James.
      b. Her name is Helen.

   3. a. He's from Albania.
      b. She's from Russia.

   4. a. No, her book is in her bag.
      b. Yes, of course it's mine.

   5. a. She's not ready yet.
      b. He's not ready to go.

3. **Practice saying the questions and answers with a partner. Be careful not to pronounce the *h* in the pronouns when you are asking the questions.**

6 SPEAKING SKILLS: Expressing Opinions

SPEAKING SKILL

When giving a presentation or talk, use the expressions below to express opinions. This will help your listeners to distinguish between points that you are presenting as facts, and points that you are presenting as your personal view.

> In my opinion, . . .
>
> Personally, I believe . . .
>
> It seems to me that . . .
>
> I think . . .
>
> I don't think . . .
>
> As far as I'm concerned, . . .
>
> If you ask me, . . .

1. Listen to the extract from a talk. What is the talk about? What points does the speaker present as opinions?

2. Listen again, which expressions do you hear?

3. Do you agree with the speaker? Share your opinions on the topic with a partner.

7 SPEAKING PRACTICE

1. Read the sentences in the chart. Note whether you agree or disagree with each sentence.

Statement	Do you agree?
A college graduate will have a better quality of life than someone who has not finished school.	
People can change their personalities.	
People are born with the personalities they have, so it doesn't matter very much how their parents raise them.	
Psychology is interesting in comparison to other subjects.	

2. Choose one of the sentences from the chart. Write some notes to yourself (a few sentences) explaining your opinion on the topic. Present your opinion to the class. Try to use one or more of the expressions in section 6 to present your view.

8 | TAKING SKILLS FURTHER

Listen to movie reviewers discuss recent films. Note what expressions they use to present their opinions. Share your observations in the next class.

For additional listening practice on the topic of psychology, go to the *Open Forum* Web site (www.oup.com/elt/openforum) and follow the links.

Topic:	Stress
Listening Texts:	Radio program on stress; interview about pet ownership
Listening Skill Focus:	Using paraphrase to work out meaning
Speaking Skill Focus:	Managing a group discussion
Vocabulary:	Collocations with verbs and prepositions
Pronunciation:	Emphasizing focus words

1 | INTRODUCING THE TOPIC

1. Work with a partner. Read the list of adjectives in the chart below. Does each adjective describe a negative feeling or a positive feeling? Check the appropriate column for each one.

Adjective	Negative feeling	Positive feeling	When might you experience these feelings?
Relaxed			
Stressed			
Anxious			
Calm			
Afraid			
Nervous			
Angry			
Focused			

2. Write down examples of when you might experience these feelings.

2 | LISTENING PRACTICE

A | Preparing to Listen

You are going to listen to a radio program about stress and its effects on the body. Before you listen, discuss these questions with a partner.

1. What are some common causes of stress in people's daily lives?

2. How does stress affect people physically?

3. How does stress impact people's emotions?

4. What are some things people can do to reduce stress?

B | Listening for Main Ideas

Listen to the program. As you listen, check your answers to the questions above. What new information did you learn from the program?

C | Listening for More Detail

Read the sentences and fill in all the information that you can. Then listen to the program again, and complete your responses. Compare your answers with a partner.

1. Confronting a situation, instead of running away or avoiding it, is an example of the

   _____ response.

2. In stressful situations, the hormones _____ and

   _____ are released, which _____ the blood

   pressure.

3. Nearly _____ percent of illness is stress-related.

4. Employers should try to reduce stress in the workplace because _____

   _____.

5. Some physical effects of stress include _____

   _____.

6. One thing we can do to reduce stress is _____

   _____.

D Focus on the Listening Skill: Using Paraphrase to Work Out Meaning

> **LISTENING SKILL**
>
> *Paraphrasing* means saying something again in different, often simpler words. Use paraphrasing to help yourself understand a complex sentence you have heard, or to identify the parts of a sentence that you do not understand. To paraphrase, break the sentence into parts. Using synonyms, rephrase the parts with simpler language. Then put the sentence back together.

1. Read and listen to this extract from the program. Pay attention to the phrases in italics. Then answer the questions.

   Excessive stress can *impair our judgment* and cause us to make mistakes in our work, possibly *jeopardizing lives.*

   1. What does *impair our judgment* mean?

      _____

   2. What does *jeopardizing lives* mean?

      _____

2. Now use your answers from exercise 1 to choose the best paraphrase for the sentence.

   _____ a. Too much stress can weaken our ability to think clearly and then cause us to make mistakes in our work, possibly putting others' lives in danger.

   _____ b. Too much stress can make us tired and cause us to make mistakes in our work that possibly affect others.

3. Listen to this second extract from the program, and answer the questions. Listen again if necessary. Then check your answers with a partner.

   1. What may family, friends and colleagues tolerate?

      _____

   2. What could happen to the relationship?

      _____

4. Use your answers to the questions in exercise 3 to help you complete the paraphrase of the extract.

   Relatives, friends, and co-workers may tolerate _____ for some time,

   but it is possible that _____.

5. Listen to the third extract and answer the questions. Listen again if necessary. Then check your answers with a partner.

1. What impact can stress have on our emotions, work, and relationships?

_____

2. What can stress do to the body's defense system? What can this lead to?

_____

3. What does research say about the relationship between stress and illness?

_____

6. Use your answers to the questions in exercise 5 to help you complete the paraphrase of the extract.

Besides acknowledging the _____ impact of stress, understanding

stress is important because _____.

According to recent research, stress causes _____.

E Thinking and Speaking

Discuss these questions in small groups or with a partner.

1. Are you less productive or more productive when you experience a little stress?
2. What causes you the most stress in your life?
3. Is there something about your lifestyle that you would like to change? If so, what? How can you change this?

3 VOCABULARY: Collocations with Verbs and Prepositions

FYI Some verbs are commonly followed by certain prepositions. For instance, the verb *depend* is usually followed by the preposition *on*, as in the sentence, "I *depend on* my brother for advice and encouragement."

1. **Read the following brochure. Would you attend this seminar?**

Do you have trouble sleeping?

It may be that you suffer from insomnia. In fact, billions of people around the world struggle with this problem. For many of them, getting a good night's rest is almost impossible. They spend countless hours lying awake at night staring at the ceiling or worrying about work, money, or other problems. In the morning, they get out of bed tired and frustrated. For many of these people, insomnia is caused by stress – stress at home, stress at work, stress anywhere in their lives. What many of these people don't know is that stress and insufficient sleep can lead to all kinds of health problems.

If you suffer from insomnia, register for this free seminar on sleep health. We'll focus on teaching you several effective ways to deal with stress-related sleep problems. These stress-relieving practices will result in better health and a better night's sleep.

z z z z Z Z Z Z

2. **Look at the list of verbs below. Read the brochure in exercise 1 again and note the preposition that is used with each verb.**

Verb	Preposition
deal	_____
focus	_____
lead	_____
register	_____
result	_____
stare	_____
struggle	_____
suffer	_____
worry	_____

3. Write a new sentence using each of the verb + preposition combinations in exercise 2.

1. _____

2. _____

3. _____

4. _____

5. _____

6. _____

7. _____

8. _____

9. _____

4 LISTENING PRACTICE

A Preparing to Listen

You are about to listen to an interview with a research scientist about the benefits of owning a pet. Before you listen, answer the questions below. Discuss your answers with a partner.

1. Almost 60% of U.S. homes have pets. Why do you think this is true? Does this surprise you? Why, or why not?

2. What are some advantages and disadvantages of owning a pet?

3. What do you think is the most popular pet in the world?

B Listening for Main Ideas

Listen to the interview. Choose the correct answer for each question.

1. What were the blood pressure results for pet owners and non-pet owners?
   a. Pet owners and non-pet owners had no difference in their blood pressure levels.
   b. People who owned dogs had lower blood pressure levels compared to non-dog owners.
   c. Getting a dog created higher blood pressure levels in new pet owners.

2. What did Dr. Yang say about pets in the workplace?
   a. They can help workers relax and be more productive.
   b. Everyone should bring a pet to work.
   c. Pets can work in the office.

3. What was NOT mentioned as a benefit of pet ownership?
   a. Having a pet is inexpensive.
   b. Having a pet can make people more physically active.
   c. Pet owners may live longer and have fewer health problems.

C Listening for More Detail

Listen to the interview again. As you listen, choose the correct answer for each question. Then compare answers with a partner. Listen again if necessary.

1. How many volunteers were used in the dog ownership study?
   a. 6
   b. 60
   c. 66

2. What were the two stressful tasks the groups had to do?
   a. Give a speech and put a hand in icy water.
   b. Give a speech and train a dog.
   c. Give a speech and measure blood pressure levels.

3. At the end of the study, which group had the higher blood pressure?
   a. The group that got dogs
   b. The group that did not get dogs
   c. Both groups had the same blood pressure levels.

4. According to Dr. Yang, what are some benefits of having a pet in the workplace?
   a. It relaxes employees and makes them more productive.
   b. It teaches employees important skills.
   c. It encourages employees to work together to care for the animal.

5. According to the interview, on average, how much longer did heart patients with pets live?
   a. About 1 month
   b. About 6 months
   c. About 1 year

6. According to the interview, when considering adopting a pet, what should people think about?
   a. The expenses that pets bring
   b. Whether their home is big enough
   c. Whether they are allergic to animals

D Thinking and Speaking

Work with a partner and discuss these questions.

1. What pets would help you be less stressed?

2. How do you think a pet could cause you more stress?

5 | PRONUNCIATION: Emphasizing Focus Words

The focus word is the most important word in a statement. Speakers emphasize focus words by stressing them. This makes the important words easier to hear and understand. Focus words are usually content words (nouns, verbs, adverbs, and adjectives).

1. Read and listen to the passage below. The focus words are in bold. Notice how they are emphasized.

Did you know that some stress is actually **good** for you? If you don't have a **little** stress in your life, it may be hard to **motivate** yourself. But how do you know what **good** stress is, and what **bad** stress is? The easiest thing to do is pay attention to how you're **feeling**. Are you **cheerful**, or **angry**? **Worried** or **content**? Are you **sleeping** well? Everyone has **different** stress levels. Pay attention to how much stress your body is **comfortable** with.

2. Listen and read the following extracts from the interview. Underline the focus words. The number in parentheses () will tell you how many focus words there are in each sentence.

1. Thank you. I'm honored to be here. (2)

2. We believe the effect is the same, regardless of the pet involved. (2)

3. Caring for an animal can be very therapeutic. (1)

4. And, it's not only stress levels that are being affected by our animal friends. (1)

5. Before getting an animal, potential pet owners need to remember that this is a long-term relationship. (2)

6. Pet owners have to be ready because it's a huge responsibility. (2)

3. Practice saying the sentences. Be sure to emphasize the focus words.

6 | SPEAKING SKILLS: Managing a Group Discussion

> **SPEAKING SKILL**
>
> When leading a group discussion, use the phrases below to focus the group members' attention, to ask the group members for opinions or suggestions, and to check for agreement.

Focusing Attention	Asking for Opinions and Suggestions	Asking for More Opinions and Suggestions	Checking for Agreement
OK, let's get started. Alright, who wants to start? So, here's the topic of our discussion. Let's get back to our topic.	Any ideas? What can we say about this? What do you think?	Anything else? Anyone have something else to add? What else can we say?	What do the rest of you think about that? Do we all agree?

1. Listen to the discussion. What are the people talking about?

2. Listen again. Notice how the discussion leader manages the discussion. What expressions do you hear?

7 | SPEAKING PRACTICE

1. Look at the different ways people lower stress. Do you ever lower your stress in these ways? For each activity write an *A* for always, an *S* for sometimes or an *N* for never.

How do you lower stress?	
1. Exercise	
2. Talk to friends	
3. Write in a journal	
4. Eat	
5. Meditate	
6. Take a nap	
7. Take a bath or shower	
9. Go out with friends	
10. Other: _____	

2. Compare your answers in groups and discuss any differences in the ways you lower stress. One student should act as a group leader.

8 | TAKING SKILLS FURTHER

Watch a cooking program or some other show in which someone is explaining how to do something. Listen for sequencing expressions and note the expressions that the speaker uses. Report your findings in the next class.

For additional listening practice on the topic of stress, go to the *Open Forum* Web site (www.oup.com/elt/openforum) and follow the links.

ABOUT THIS CHAPTER

Topics:	Management principles; entrepreneurship
Listening Texts:	Lecture on management principles; informal talk at a business association
Listening Skill Focus:	Identifying pronoun reference
Speaking Skill Focus:	Preparing for a presentation
Vocabulary:	Words related to management
Pronunciation:	Using stress to show contrast

1 | INTRODUCING THE TOPIC

Work with a partner. Look at the newspaper ads and answer the questions below.

Certified Nurse Needed
to provide home care to patients throughout the state.

Minimum 3 years experience required.

Must have own car and be willing to travel.

Benefits include paid vacation and flexible hours.

Well-established Law Firm seeking enthusiastic general assistant.

Must have excellent communication skills,

basic computer skills, and type 30 words per minute.

Prior experience required.

Bilingual skills preferred.

1. Would either of these jobs interest you? Why?

2. What kind of education or experience do you think these jobs require?

3. What is your dream job? Why does that job interest you?

A Preparing to Listen

1. Look at the following list of characteristics. Which do you think are the most important characteristics of a good boss or manager? Are any of these negative characteristics for a boss or manager?

   A good manager or boss . . .

   _____ is a positive role model

   _____ is a leader

   _____ knows the strengths of the employees

   _____ closely observes the performance of employees

   _____ sets high standards and does not tolerate mistakes

   _____ has good communication skills

   _____ devotes all his or her time to work

   _____ openly criticizes employees

2. Compare your choices with a partner. Are they the same? If not, discuss the differences.

B Listening for Main Ideas

Listen to a lecture on principles of good management. Circle the characteristics above that the speaker mentions as important for a good manager. Compare answers with a partner.

C Listening for More Detail

Read the questions and answer the ones you can. Then listen to the lecture again and note your answers as you listen. Compare answers with a partner. Listen again if necessary.

1. Who are most of the people in the audience? _____

   _____

2. What are two examples of managers who are good role models? _____

   _____

   _____

3. How does a good manager know the strengths of his or her employees? _____

_____

_____

4. How should managers support employees? _____

_____

_____

5. How do good managers deal with mistakes? _____

_____

_____

6. What is the speaker's feeling about managers and a personal life? _____

_____

_____

7. What suggestions does the speaker offer for workers who have bad managers?

_____

_____

D Focus on the Listening Skill: Identifying Pronoun Reference

> **LISTENING SKILL**
>
> Pronouns refer to a specific word or words in the same sentence or in a previous sentence. When listening to someone speak, it's important to understand which word(s) pronouns are being used to refer to.

1. **Read and listen to this extract. Then identify which word(s) each pronoun in bold refers to.**

Good managers are good role models for employees. (1) **They** understand a company's beliefs and (2) **its** mission, and (3) **they** tend to lead by example. As a result, good managers earn the respect of the people (4) **they** supervise and help (5) **them** become leaders, too.

1. Here, *they* refers to _____.
   a. good managers
   b. employees

2. Here, *its* refers to _____.
   a. employees'
   b. a company's

3. Here, *they* refers to _____.
   a. good managers
   b. employees

4. Here, *they* refers to _____.
   a. good managers
   b. employees

5. Here, *them* refers to _____.
   a. good managers
   b. employees

2. **Read and listen to this extract. Fill in the missing pronouns.**

We see here another characteristic of effective managers. Effective managers see the unique strengths of (1) _____ employees and try to utilize those strengths in (2) _____ organization. This kind of manager observes what tasks (3) _____ or (4) _____ people do well, what responsibilities (5) _____ learn quickly, and which of (6) _____ (7) _____ enjoy doing. And a good manager will reward (8) _____ by giving (9) _____ tasks that encourage the use of these skills.

3. **Work with a partner to identify who or what each pronoun refers to.**

E Thinking and Speaking

Work in small groups. Discuss these questions.

1. Have you ever worked with a bad manager or group leader? What difficulties did you face? How did you resolve the situation?

2. Do you believe bad managers can change? If so, how?

3 VOCABULARY: Words Related to Management

1. Read the passage below, paying attention to the words and expressions in bold.

My first teaching experience was wonderful because I had a great **supervisor**. At first I was intimidated by her because she was such an experienced, dedicated, and energetic teacher. However, she turned out to be the perfect **role model** for me. I learned so much just by watching her teach and interact with her students. She also did a wonderful job of **mentoring** me. For instance, we would often discuss the challenges I was facing at work, and she would give me advice about how to overcome and learn from those challenges. One thing I really appreciated is how she helped me **set objectives** for myself and my students, and then she helped me stay focused on those goals. In our weekly meetings, she would always ask thoughtful questions. She would also **provide feedback** on my performance. I always appreciated this because I wanted to know whether or not I was doing a good job.

Some of the other new teachers weren't so fortunate. I remember one had a supervisor who was always **micro-managing** his teachers. He basically tried to control everything the teachers did in the classroom and didn't allow them any opportunity to experiment or try new ideas. Another was matched with an aggressive supervisor who could only be described as a **bully**. She would put unnecessary pressure on teachers and sometimes even yell at them.

I'm just glad I had Mrs. Henderson because she had a truly positive impact on the development of my teaching skills. She taught me to patiently guide my students and co-exist with my **colleagues** – the other teachers. She also taught me specific skills that are useful in any job. For instance when I first started teaching, I tried to do too much of the **departmental** work on my own. Mrs. Henderson **trained** me to **delegate** some of those tasks to others, so I wouldn't have to do them all myself. She also helped me develop important **time management** skills, and this has helped me tremendously throughout my career. Because of her, my first experiences as a teacher were positive ones, and I can truly say that she **motivated** me to be the teacher I am today.

2. Match each word or expression with the correct definition.

__l__	1. mentor	a. someone who uses their power to hurt or frighten others
____	2. delegate	b. try to control every little detail of employees' work
____	3. set objectives	c. connected with a department
____	4. micro-manage	d. identify goals
____	5. role model	e. teach a person the skills for a job
____	6. colleagues	f. make someone want to do something
____	7. bully	g. offer comment
____	8. departmental	h. someone in charge of other employees in a workplace
____	9. motivate	i. give part of your work to someone else
____	10. train	j. person you admire and try to copy
____	11. provide feedback	k. people you work with; co-workers
____	12. time management	l. advise and help somebody with less experience
____	13. supervisor	m. the ability to use time wisely and get tasks done efficiently

3. **Work with a partner. Choose two or three of the following topics to discuss with your partner. Tell your partner about your experiences or thoughts on the topic.**

   • Someone who was an important role model for you

   • An example of someone you know who micro-manages

   • The effect or impact a bully can have on someone

   • Experiences you've had mentoring someone

4 | LISTENING PRACTICE

A Preparing to Listen

1. Work with a partner. Look at the graph and discuss the questions.

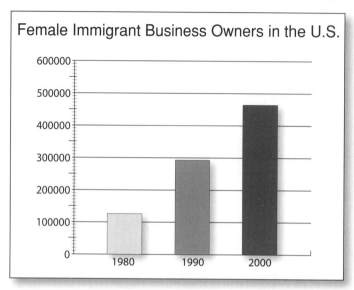

1. In 1980, approximately how many business owners in the United States were female immigrants? How many female immigrant business owners were there in 2000?

2. Why do you think the number of female immigrant business owners has increased so rapidly?

B Listening for Main Ideas

Listen to a presentation to a local business group. As you listen, number the main ideas in the order they are presented.

_____ a. The number of female immigrant entrepreneurs has increased drastically since 1980.

_____ b. Many of these business owners need more business training and more cultural understanding.

_____ c. One of the challenges these women face is raising enough money to start and maintain a business.

_____ d. Some immigrant women begin their own businesses because they have few other options for employment.

_____ e. These women are making a great impact on their communities and the economy.

C Listening for More Detail

Listen again. Write *T* for true or *F* for false for each statement. Compare answers with a partner. Listen again if necessary.

_____ 1. Fifty years ago, in the United States, it was more common for a male to own a small business or manufacturing company.

_____ 2. Although female immigrant entrepreneurs have increased, there are still more native-born female entrepreneurs.

_____ 3. Economics and a desire for independence are some of the reasons immigrant women enter the business field.

_____ 4. Female immigrant entrepreneurs contribute to the community by employing others and by serving as role models.

_____ 5. Getting funding is no longer a problem for female immigrants going into business.

_____ 6. Connie, the speaker from Mexico, owned a bakery in Mexico.

_____ 7. Kim started a dog grooming center.

_____ 8. Lan doesn't need to work, but she likes getting out of the house and talking with other women.

D Thinking and Speaking

Work with a partner and discuss these questions.

1. Would you prefer to own your own business or work for a company or organization owned by someone else?

2. What do you think are some of the benefits of owning your own business?

3. What are some possible drawbacks to owning your own business?

5 | PRONUNCIATION: Using Stress to Show Contrast

FYI Speakers often stress certain words to indicate a contrast between words.

1. Read and listen to the extract. Notice how the words in bold are stressed. Why do you think the speaker stresses these words?

Owning your own business—working for **yourself,** instead of someone **else**—has long been part of the American dream.

🎧 2. Read the following extract and underline the words you think should be stressed to show contrast. Then listen and check your answers.

The number of immigrant female entrepreneurs has recently surpassed the number of native-born female entrepreneurs. In fact they are expected to soon challenge the number of immigrant male entrepreneurs.

3. Work with a partner and practice saying the extracts in exercise 1 and exercise 2.

6 | SPEAKING SKILLS: Preparing for a Presentation

> **SPEAKING SKILL**
>
> It is important to plan and prepare well for a presentation. This will help you feel more confident and relaxed when you present. Once you've chosen a topic for your presentation, the steps below can help you organize your thoughts and get ready for the presentation.

1. Work with a partner and discuss these questions.

   1. Have you ever given a presentation to a large or small audience? If so, how did you prepare?

   2. If you had to do it again, how would you prepare differently?

2. One way to prepare for a presentation is to use note cards. Here are some steps that many people follow when using note cards for a presentation. Put them in logical order. Compare answers with a partner.

   _____ List one or two ideas from your outline on each note card, using symbols and abbreviations to remind you of what you want to say. Only use full sentences for quotations.

   _____ Ask your friends for feedback after your first practice. Write down the feedback you receive.

   _____ Make sure each note card has a number on it, so you know the order in which each idea should be presented.

   _____ Read over your note cards and use a highlighter to indicate points that are especially important.

   _____ Practice giving your presentation in front of friends and/or a video camera. Time yourself to make sure the presentation is not too long or too short.

   __1__ Create an outline for your presentation.

   _____ Make sure to get enough sleep on the night before your presentation and show up early to the place where you will present.

   _____ Practice again. Try to look at your audience while you speak, and only glance quickly at the cards as a reminder.

3. Discuss these questions with a partner.

1. Have you used note cards when making presentations? How are they helpful?

2. Why would you use symbols or abbreviations on your note cards, instead of full sentences?

3. What problems might you encounter when using note cards to give a presentation? How can you avoid these problems?

7 | SPEAKING PRACTICE

1. Choose one of the following topics, or a topic of your own, and prepare a short presentation. Use note cards and the steps for preparing in section 6.

- The skills needed to be a successful entrepreneur

- How to choose a career

- How to prepare for a career in a particular field

- The skills needed to be a successful student

2. Take turns giving your presentation for the class.

8 | TAKING SKILLS FURTHER

Outside of class, list some additional steps that you can follow to prepare for a presentation. Think about different presentation settings and how you might prepare for each one. Compare your ideas in the next class.

 For additional listening practice on the topic of business, go to the *Open Forum* Web site (www.oup.com/elt/openforum) and follow the links.

ABOUT THIS CHAPTER	
Topic:	Space tourism and exploration
Listening Texts:	Radio report on space tourism; on-the-street survey about space exploration
Listening Skill Focus:	Identifying technical language
Speaking Skill Focus:	Conducting surveys
Vocabulary:	Metaphorical language
Pronunciation:	Linking

1 | INTRODUCING THE TOPIC

1. Work with a partner and try to answer the questions in the quiz. (The answers are at the bottom of the page.)

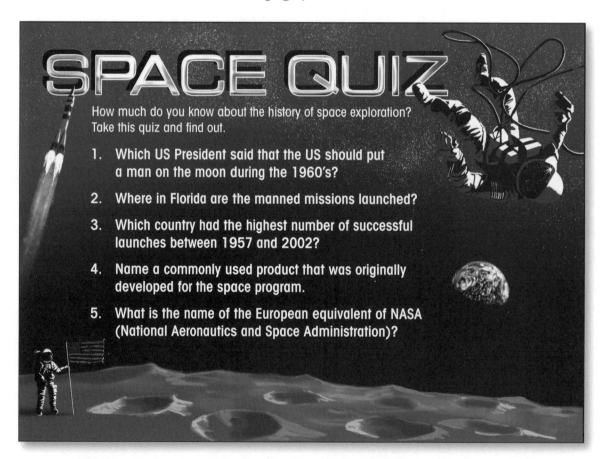

SPACE QUIZ

How much do you know about the history of space exploration? Take this quiz and find out.

1. Which US President said that the US should put a man on the moon during the 1960's?

2. Where in Florida are the manned missions launched?

3. Which country had the highest number of successful launches between 1957 and 2002?

4. Name a commonly used product that was originally developed for the space program.

5. What is the name of the European equivalent of NASA (National Aeronautics and Space Administration)?

2. Check your answers to the quiz. How many questions did you answer correctly? Did any of the answers surprise you?

Answers: 1. John F. Kennedy 2. Cape Canaveral 3. Russia 4. Many answers are possible, including freeze dried food, bar codes, cordless tools, Velcro; 5. ESA (European Space Agency)

A Preparing to Listen

1. Work in small groups. Look at the following advertisement and answer the questions.

1. What do you think this advertisement is promoting?

2. Why do you think the company is called Stellar Excursions?

3. Would you be interested in the services provided by Stellar Excursions?

2. Compare your answers as a class.

B Listening for Main Ideas

Listen to the radio program. Then number the topics below in the order they are mentioned.

_____ a. Reasons people might want to visit space

_____ b. The first space tourist

_____ c. The cost of space tourism

_____ d. The development of orbiting hotels

_____ e. How NASA feels about space tourism

C Listening for More Detail

🎧 Listen to the program again. Write *T* for true or *F* for false for each statement.

_____ 1. Dennis Tito is a Japanese businessman who became an astronaut.

_____ 2. There has never been enough space for tourists on a NASA space shuttle flight.

_____ 3. The biggest problem for space tourism is the high cost of launching vehicles.

_____ 4. Launching vehicles are destroyed with each launch.

_____ 5. If there is a sharp increase in the number of paying customers, the cost of space travel could decrease by as much as 70%.

_____ 6. Orbiting hotels will probably be luxurious.

_____ 7. The development and maintenance of services will be important to travelers.

D Thinking and Speaking

Work in small groups. Discuss these questions.

1. Would you consider space travel if you could afford it?

2. What concerns would you have about traveling into space?

E Focus on the Listening Skill: Identifying Technical Language

> **LISTENING SKILL**
>
> It is useful to identify and define technical language to help you understand a report or a lecture. You can then use the technical language in your summaries and discussion.

1. Listen to the radio program again and write down any technical terms you hear. Then compare your list of words with a partner. Can you work out the meaning of the words?

2. Look at the list of technical terms in the box. Match each term with a definition below. Compare your answers with a partner.

launching vehicle	orbit	space shuttle
cosmonauts	solar system	space station
satellite	atmosphere	

1 ___launching vehicle___ :   something used to get off the ground and into space

2 _____ :   space crafts that can be reused to travel back and forth over a distance

3 _____ : move in a path around another body

4 _____ : astronauts from Russia

5 _____ : large structure that can house a crew of scientists in space for a long period of time

6 _____ : a structure that travels around a planet or a moon

7 _____ : the sun and the planets that travel around it

8 _____ : the layer of gas that surrounds the earth or another planet

F Thinking and Speaking

Work in pairs. Create a short radio or TV advertisement promoting a space travel excursion. Present your ad to another pair. Compare and note similarities and differences. What key elements did both pairs include?

3 VOCABULARY: Metaphorical Language

1. Read and listen to the extracts from the program. Pay attention to the words and expressions in italics. Choose the correct meaning for each word or expression. Then compare answers with a partner.

   1. People have been *buzzing* about the possibility of space tourism.

      Here *buzzing* probably means _____.
      a. making a humming sound
      b. talking a lot about a topic

   2. The first moon landing was a *monumental* accomplishment.

      Here *monumental* probably means _____.
      a. like a statue or other memorial
      b. important and memorable

   3. *Exploding* tourism will spark the development of many new, imaginative services, constructions, and activities in the hospitality industry.

      Here *exploding* probably means _____.
      a. spreading and growing quickly
      b. bursting or breaking apart violently

   4. Because of their high cost, these tours are still *out of reach* for most people.

      Here *out of reach* probably means _____.
      a. not possible
      b. too far away

5. Astronauts have reported that the views of earth from outer space are *out of this world.*

Here *out of this world* probably means _____.
   a. from another planet
   b. amazing

2. **Complete the sentences with expressions from exercise 1.**

1. The beaches in Hawaii are absolutely _____.

2. The office is _____ about the changes in management.

3. The discovery of penicillin was a _____ achievement in medical history.

4. I tried as hard as I could, but the 1st place prize was just _____.

5. After a summer rainstorm, the desert will _____ with color as flowers pop up everywhere.

4 LISTENING PRACTICE

A Preparing to Listen

Discuss these questions in pairs or groups.

1. What are some reasons for exploring outer space?

2. How have we benefited from space exploration?

3. What are some concerns people may have about spending money on the exploration of outer space?

B Listening for Main Ideas

🎧 Listen to an on-the-street survey about space exploration. As you listen, check the three main topics that are discussed. (All the topics are mentioned.)

_____ a. The first moon landing

_____ b. Benefits of ocean exploration

_____ c. Concern about cost

_____ d. Benefits of the space program

_____ e. History of the space program

C Listening for More Detail

🎧 Read the questions below. Then listen to the survey again. Choose the correct answer to complete each item. Then compare answers with a partner. Listen again if necessary.

1. Instead of sending astronauts into space, one man suggests _____.
   a. sending animals
   b. sending robots

2. One man thinks our first priority before spending money on space exploration should be to _____.
   a. help the unemployed and the homeless
   b. explore the ocean

3. Bar codes, smoke detectors, cordless power tools, and rescue cutters were all created _____.
   a. for space
   b. in space

4. By studying Venus, scientists hope to find out more about _____.
   a. what causes global warming
   b. how to live on other planets

D Thinking and Speaking

Work in pairs or in small groups. Look at the pictures and discuss the questions.

Identify the items above. Which items have you used and how useful do you think they are? Which ones save lives?

5 | PRONUNCIATION: Linking

When a word ending in a consonant sound is followed by a word that begins with the same consonant sound, English speakers often link the words together so that the consonant sound is pronounced only once, but slightly longer than usual. For example, the words *last time* usually sound like "lastime." This is a natural feature of spoken language, but it can make it hard to hear where one word ends and the other begins.

1. Listen to the words and notice how they are linked. How do you think this affects listening?

   first⌢time

   space⌢station

   real⌢life

   touched⌢down

2. Repeat the words to yourself, linking them together.

3. Listen to the sentences and write the missing words in the blanks.

   1. That was the _____ someone landed on the moon.

   2. Did your _____ you at the airport?

   3. We don't have enough _____.

   4. We had to _____ a rainstorm.

   5. They _____ close to each other.

   6. Our _____ one year to orbit the sun.

4. Practice saying the sentences, linking the words you wrote down.

6 | SPEAKING SKILLS: Conducting a Survey

SPEAKING SKILL

When conducting a survey, it is important to introduce yourself and then get right to the point. It's customary to start with a polite introduction explaining the purpose of the survey, and then go directly to the questions. Try using the introductions below when you are conducting a survey.

Hello. We're trying to find out . . . Would you mind answering some questions?
Hi, would you mind if I asked you a few questions about . . . ?
Excuse me. I'm conducting a brief survey. Could I ask you what you think about . . . ?
Excuse me. Do you have a moment to answer a few questions about . . . ?

1. Listen to someone conducting a survey about the best way to relax on the weekend.

2. Listen again. How does the speaker introduce himself? Does he get to the questions quickly enough? Does he ask too many questions?

7 | SPEAKING PRACTICE

1. Work in small groups. Choose one of the topics below and write 3 or 4 survey questions about it. Then take turns surveying the other students in your group. Try to use some of the introductory expressions from section 6.

   • Your opinion on global warming
   • Your opinion about whether the world should use one common currency
   • Your ideas on making English the national language in the U.S.
   • Your opinion on creating prisons in outer space

2. Discuss the following questions in your groups.

   1. Which expressions did you use to introduce yourself before asking your questions?

   2. Do you feel comfortable with these expressions? If not, discuss ways you can make them feel more natural.

8 | TAKING SKILLS FURTHER

Conduct your own survey outside of class. Use questions from the surveys you listened to or select another topic from section 7 and create your own questions. Ask some people you don't know to answer the questions. Report your findings in the next class.

For additional listening practice on the topic of space exploration, go to the *Open Forum* Web site (www.oup.com/elt/openforum) and follow the links.

ABOUT THIS CHAPTER	
Topics:	Forensic archaeology; Hatshepsut
Listening Texts:	Radio interview with a forensic archaeologist; college lecture about Hatshepsut
Listening Skill Focus:	Identifying expressions of uncertainty
Speaking Skill Focus:	Asking for more details
Vocabulary:	Words related to archaeology
Pronunciation:	The *–ed* ending

1 | INTRODUCING THE TOPIC

1. Work in small groups. Look at the photograph of archaeologists at work and discuss the questions.

1. What are these archaeologists doing?

2. What do archaeologists study?

3. What can we learn from archaeology?

4. What kinds of challenges do archaeologists face?

2 LISTENING PRACTICE

A Preparing to Listen

Look at the following description of a radio program. What is the program about? What do you think a forensic archaeologist does?

Thursday 8:30

Spotlight with Steve Jensen

Steve will be talking with Dr. Roland Jeffries, forensic archaeologist, about how the smallest details can help solve even the most complex criminal mysteries

B Listening for Main Ideas

Listen to the interview and answer the questions. Compare answers with a partner.

1. How can archaeologists help solve crimes? _____

_____

2. What kinds of difficulties do forensic archaeologists encounter?_____

_____

C Listening for More Detail

Listen to the interview again. Write *T* for true or *F* for false for each statement. Compare answers with a partner. Listen again if necessary.

_____ 1. Forensic archaeologists study bones and hair to discover when a person died.

_____ 2. Forensic archaeologists can determine the exact time that a person died.

_____ 3. Forensic archaeologists can determine if a person had a sports injury or suffered from domestic violence.

_____ 4. The forensic archaeologist is often bored by his work.

_____ 5. Kennewick Man was found in 1896.

_____ 6. Native Americans feel studying the dead is disrespectful.

D Focus on the Listening Skill: Identifying Expressions of Uncertainty

> **LISTENING SKILL**
>
> When you listen to someone speak, it's important to notice whether the speaker is completely certain about the information he or she is sharing. When speakers are not sure if what they are saying is accurate, they will sometimes use expressions like the ones below to show uncertainty.

> I guess . . .
> I think . . .
> It seems . . .
> It appears that . . .
> It could be that . . .
> I believe that . . .
> Maybe . . .
> We can't be certain, but . . .
> We don't know for sure, but . . .

1. Listen to extracts from the interview. Decide whether the speaker is expressing certainty or uncertainty about the information he is presenting. Circle the correct answer.

   1. certainty   uncertainty

   2. certainty   uncertainty

   3. certainty   uncertainty

   4. certainty   uncertainty

   5. certainty   uncertainty

2. Listen to the sentences again. Which words helped you decide whether the speaker is expressing uncertainty.

E Thinking and Speaking

Work with a partner and discuss these questions.

1. Do you know of any important discoveries made by archaeologists?

2. Have you ever seen an important archaeological artifact? Explain your answer.

1. **Read the paragraphs, paying attention to the words in bold.**

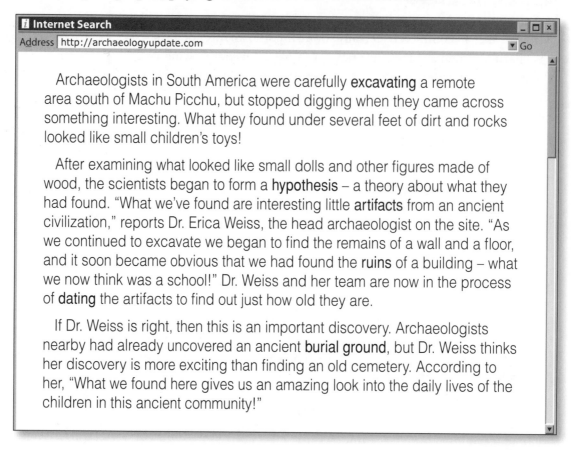

2. **Fill in the blanks with the correct form of the words in bold from exercise 1.**

1. They are currently using heavy machinery to _____ the area. We'll see what they find when they finish digging.

2. We haven't formed a _____ yet, but we expect to figure out what happened here soon.

3. Based on the evidence we've gathered, it seems that this area was used as a

   _____ for dead members of royalty.

4. Some archaeologists have been known to steal precious _____ from archaeological sites.

5. Scientists accidentally stumbled upon the _____ of an ancient temple. All that was left were some pillars and pieces of the floor.

6. According to reports, the temple _____ back to 100 BC.

A Preparing to Listen

1. You are going to hear a college lecture about a ruler of ancient Egypt. Before listening, read the following facts about ancient Egypt.

    1. The king of Egypt was called pharaoh.
    2. Brothers and sisters sometimes married to continue the royal bloodline.
    3. Rulers of ancient Egypt built elaborate monuments.
    4. Women enjoyed many of the same rights as men did.
    5. Egyptians believed in an afterlife.

2. Are any of the facts surprising to you? If so, which ones? Discuss your answers with a partner.

B Listening for Main Ideas

Listen to the college lecture. Choose the correct ending for each statement.

1. Hatshepsut was a _____.
    a. queen
    b. pharaoh

2. While Hatshepsut was in power, Egypt _____.
    a. prospered
    b. declined

3. Hatshepsut's death _____.
    a. was the result of murder
    b. is still a mystery

C Listening for More Detail

Read the questions and answer the ones you can. Then listen to the lecture again and finish answering the questions. Compare answers with a partner. Listen again if necessary.

1. Who did Hatshepsut marry? _____

   _____

   _____

2. After she came to the throne, what did she slowly start doing? _____

   _____

   _____

3. How did she explain her right to be pharaoh? _____

   _____

   _____

4. Name two projects that she carried out. _____

   _____

   _____

5. What is located at Deir el-Bahri? _____

   _____

   _____

6. Why is this building important? _____

   _____

   _____

7. What happened to many of Hatshepsut's images?_____

   _____

   _____

8. What did ancient Egyptians believe about the afterlife? _____

   _____

   _____

9. What happened to Hatshepsut? _____

_____

_____

10. When was the Red Chapel built? _____

_____

_____

D Working Out Unknown Vocabulary

Listen to the extracts from the lecture. Listen for the words and expressions in italics. Choose the correct meaning for each word or expressions. Then compare answers with a partner. Discuss the reasons for your choices.

1. *Reigned* probably means _____.
   a. lived, existed
   b. governed, ruled

2. *Depicted* probably means _____.
   a. performed
   b. represented

3. *Divine* probably means _____.
   a. god like
   b. legal

4. *Intact* probably means _____.
   a. undiscovered, hidden
   b. whole, complete

5. *Vandalism* probably means _____.
   a. destruction of property
   b. created

6. *In obscurity* probably means _____.
   a. unknown
   b. popular, famous

E Thinking and Speaking

Work with a partner and discuss these questions.

1. Why do you think Hatshepsut's image was destroyed?

2. What women politicians do you know of? What positions do they hold?

3. Are there any differences between male and female leaders? If so, what are they?

5 PRONUNCIATION: The –ed ending

FYI

The –ed ending at the end of a verb can be pronounced three different ways, depending on the verb it is used with.

If the last sound of a verb is /t/ or /d/, the –ed is pronounced /ɪd/. This adds an extra syllable to the verb. For instance, the verb *waited* sounds like "waitid."

If a verb ends in a voiced sound (other than /d/), the –ed ending is pronounced /d/. For instance, the verb *sneezed* sounds like "sneezd."

If a verb ends in a voiceless sound (other than /t/), the –ed ending is pronounced /t/. For instance, the word *stopped* sounds like "stopt."

1. Look at the list of verbs. Decide how the –ed ending should be pronounced with each verb.

	/ɪd/	/d/	/t/
1. ask	____	____	____
2. love	____	____	____
3. drop	____	____	____
4. explain	____	____	____
5. relate	____	____	____
6. compare	____	____	____
7. enjoy	____	____	____
8. omit	____	____	____
9. believe	____	____	____
10. survive	____	____	____
11. note	____	____	____
12. locate	____	____	____

2. Listen to the verbs with the –ed ending and check your answers.

3. Listen to these sentences, paying attention to the words in italics. Then practice saying the sentences with a partner. Be sure to pronounce the –ed ending correctly.

1. My nephew *wanted* to go to the museum.

2. We *waited* for the bus for 30 minutes.

3. We *arrived* at the museum around 9:30.

4. We *watched* a short film about ancient Egypt.

5. We *walked* around the exhibits.

6. We *looked* at everything.

7. He *loved* every minute of it.

8. It *turned* out to be a wonderful day.

6 | SPEAKING SKILL: Asking for More Details

SPEAKING SKILL

Don't be afraid to ask for more details during a class or a conversation. The expressions below can help you ask for more specific details about a particular topic.

> Can you tell me more about . . . ?
> Could you go into more detail about . . . ?
> Can you be a bit more specific about . . . ?
> I'd love to hear more about . . .

1. Listen to the extracts from a classroom lecture. What do the students want to know more about?

2. Listen again. Which expressions do they use to ask for more details?

7 | SPEAKING PRACTICE

Work with a partner. Act out the following role play situations. Take turns as Student A and Student B.

Role Play 1

Student A: Pretend you missed the last class. Ask Student B to tell you about what was covered in the class you missed. Be sure to ask for specific details about the lesson, class discussions, homework, etc. Use some of the expressions above to ask for specific details.

Student B: Answer Student A's questions. Do not present all the details at once. Instead, allow Student A to ask for specific information.

Role Play 2

Student A: Ask Student B to tell you about his or her favorite historical figure (favorite person in history). Continue asking for specific details about the person until you can guess who he or she is.

Student B: Don't tell Student A the name of your favorite historical figure. Instead, tell Student A about the person (for instance, when and where he/she lived, why he/she is famous, why you admire him/her, etc.) until your partner can guess who the person is.

8 | TAKING SKILLS FURTHER

Work with a partner or small group. Visit a retirement center or an elementary school to explain something unique from your culture. Make note of the questions or expressions your listeners use to ask for more details. Report on your experience in the next class.

For additional listening practice on the topic of archaeology, go to the *Open Forum* Web site (www.oup.com/elt/openforum) and follow the links.